# INTERACTIVE ENGLISH 1



## MANOJ PUBLICATIONS

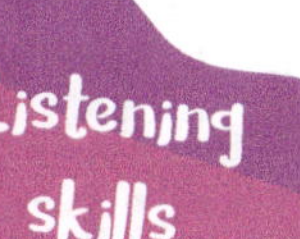

# Interactive English-1


**Publishers:**

**MANOJ PUBLICATIONS**

761, Main Road, Burari, Delhi-110084 (INDIA)

Mobile : 09999476076, 09868112194,
08178823569, 08178854810

Email : info@manojpublications.com

**For online shopping visit our website :**

Website : www.sawanonlinebookstore.com

ISBN : 978-93-5579-205-1

*Concept by:*
**Sanyam Gupta**

*Edited by:*
**Rohan Kumar**

# PREFACE

Effective communication in a language requires a deep knowledge of its grammatical structure, an enriched vocabulary bank, reading and listening, comprehension and sound writing skills in various formats.

Grammar serves as a binder of the various language skills and needs to be learnt in a contextualised manner. It should enable the learners to make connections with their environment and give voice to their expressions in a grammatically correct way.

The present series entitled Interactive English offers a paradigm shift in the teaching of grammar.

Its hands-on approach is in tandem with a time-tested methodology and its real-life application. The syllabus coverage is fine-tuned to the most recent guidelines of NEP (National Education Policy).

The series serves as a platform for the learners to master the language along with its communicative approach.

The concepts and sub-concepts covered in the series are carefully evaluated to cater for the most demanding needs of the learners. The explanations and the examples have been given in an understandable language. An effort has been made to link learning with the immediate and the not-so-immediate surroundings of the learner.

Each concept has its own practice task. The tasks at the end of each chapter are integrated and include traditional exercises. Moreover, from Class 3 onwards, Aural-Oral activities to reinforce the learners' acquired knowledge have been included.

The series gives due importance to vocabulary building, comprehension of the written and spoken words and writing skills to attain a finer understanding of the language. The learners are sensitised to common errors in the use of grammatical structures in order to promote self-learning.

Each chapter includes a task that is open-ended and is meant to hone the thinking and analytical skills of the learners. The revision papers are placed at regular intervals to assess the progress of the learners, be it self-assessment or an assessment done by the teachers.

The series gives a holistic view of learning and teaching a language. It combines grammar with the essential language skills as well as thinking skills.

Last but not least, teachers' manual adopts a hands-on approach that promises to be an asset to the teaching fraternity.

– Author

# CONTENTS

# 1 Little Jimmy

**Look at the given pictures and answer the questions:**

1. Which animal do you see in the picture?

   ___________________________________

2. How many children are playing in the park?

   ___________________________________

3. What is the colour of the house?

   ___________________________________

Jimmy is a little boy. He has a puppy named Benny. It is his first day to school. His mother tells him to pack his bag. His father tells him not to play with Benny anymore.

Jimmy packs his bag. He goes to school by bus. He reaches school and makes many friends. But he misses his puppy Benny. He rushes home when school gets over.

Benny and Jimmy get ready to go to the park. Jimmy looks for Benny's red ball. He cannot find it. He searches for it everywhere. Benny sniffs around. He barks loudly sniffing Jimmy's bag. The ball is inside Jimmy's bag. Jimmy takes it out. Benny barks in happiness. They go the park and play with the red ball.

## A. Choose the correct word to fill up each blank:

1. It is Jimmy's _____________ day to school. (first/last)

2. Benny is Jimmy's _____________. (puppy/cat)

3. Jimmy cannot find the _____________. (bat/ball)

4. Jimmy and Benny go to the _____________ to play. (park/garden)

5. Jimmy's mother tell him to pack his _____________. (box/bag)

6. Jimmy's father tells him not to play with _____________.

(Benny/ball)

**B. Put a (✓) for 'True' and (✗) for 'False' in the boxes:**

1. Jimmy has a cat. ☐
2. Benny is a puppy. ☐
3. Jimmy goes to the market. ☐
4. Benny has a red ball. ☐
5. Jimmy cannot find the bat. ☐

**WORD POWER**

**C. Complete the sentences using words from the box:**

> pencil   bicycle   red   love

1. The boy writes with a ____________________.

2. Sita wears a ____________________ dress.

3. John rides his ____________________.

4. Parents ____________________ us very much.

**D. Rearrange the letters to make meaningfull words:**

1. W T E A R       ____________________

2. S N U       ____________________

3. B T O S O       ____________________

4. C L U D O       ____________________

5. I C E P N L       ____________________

A group of words that is complete and makes sense is called a **sentence**.

**For example:**

Jennifer my best is friend (It is not a sentence)

Jennifer is my best friend. (It is a sentence)

**E.    Put in the box (✓) if it is a sentence and (✗) if it is not:**

1. Rain is ☐

2. The cat drinks milk. ☐

3. Sam rides a horse. ☐

4. The tall giraffe ☐

5. The lion roars loudly. ☐

6. A sleepy cat ☐

7. Elephant is ☐

8. The bird is flying. ☐

**F.    Look at the pictures below and say their names aloud:**

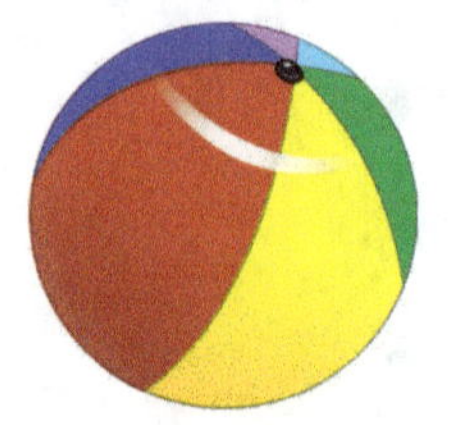   

 **Let's read aloud:**

1. Harry is wearing a <u>hat</u>.
2. He <u>sat</u> on a <u>mat</u>.
3. He looks <u>sad</u>.
4. He is <u>mad</u>.

Each of the underlined words has a similar sound. This is the sound of 'a'. Think of more words that have the sound of 'a'.

**THINK AND TELL**

**H. Choose the correct option and complete the sentences:**

1. We play in the _________________.

    a. park            b. road            c. shop

2. A doctor works in a _________________.

    a. school          b. hospital          c. office

3. A teacher teaches in a _________________.

    a. shop            b. school          c. hospital

4. We go to school to _________________.

    a. sleep           b. talk            c. learn

**LET'S WRITE**

**I. Do you know how to write letters?**

**Fill up the blanks with the missing capital letters:**

A ___ C D E ___ G H ___ J K L ___ N ___ P Q R S ___ U V W X ___ Z

**Now write A to Z by yourself:**

_______________________________________________

**Fill up the blanks with the missing small letters:**

a b c d ____ ____ g h i j ____ ____ m n o ____ ____

r s t u ____ w ____ y ____

**Now write a to z by yourself:**

__________________________________________________________

Out of the 26 letters, five are called **vowels**. These are: a, e, i, o and u.

**J.    Fill up each box with a, e, i, o or u:**

raven    butterfly    fox    cow    elephant    tiger

f [ ] x

c [ ] w

t [ ] g [ ] r

r [ ] v [ ] n

[ ] l [ ] p h [ ] n t

b [ ] t t [ ] r f l y

**ACTIVITY**

**Who am I?**

**Paste a photograph of yourself in the box given below and fill up the blanks with appropriate answers:**

My name is __________________________________________.

I am ____________ years old.

I love to play games like ______________________________

______________________________.

# The Old Woman Who Lived in a Shoe

There was an old woman
  Who lived in a shoe.

She had fifteen children,
  And loved them all too.
    She had so many children,
      She didn't know what to do

She said, "Thank you, God,
  For sending them bread."
    Then kissed them all gladly
      And sent them to bed.

### READ AND TELL

**A.**  **Fill up the blanks with the correct options:**

1. The old woman lived in a/an ___________________.

   a. apartment                                 b. shoe

2. The old woman lived with __________________.

   a. her children                              b. alone

3. The children ate __________________.

   a. bread                                     b. cheese

4. The old woman had __________________ children.

   a. thirteen                                  b. fifteen

When we are talking about an object that is near by, we use **'this'**. When the object is far away, we use **'that'**.

**For example:**
**This** is my car. **That** is my neighbour's car.

When there is more than one object **near by**, we use **'these'**. When there is more than one object **far away**, we use **'those'**.

**For example:**
**These** are my books. **Those** are my friend's books.

**B.** **Fill up the blanks with 'This' and 'That':**

1. ________ is a car. ________ is a bicycle.

2. ________ is a monkey. ________ is a banana tree.

3. ________ is a boy. ________ is a girl.

**C.** **Look at the pictures and answer the questions using 'This', 'That', 'These' and 'Those':**

1. What is that?

   ____________ is a cat.

2. What is this?

   ____________ is a pencil.

3. What are those?

   ____________ are clouds.

4. What are these?

___________ are books.

5. What is that?

___________ is an aeroplane.

6. What is this?

___________ is a car.



**D. Tick (✓) the things the children should do to help the Old Woman keep their house neat and clean:**

1. They should pick up all the toys. ☐

2. They should scatter their clothes. ☐

3. They should make all the beds neatly. ☐

4. They should not clean the dishes. ☐

5. They should wipe their shoes before entering the house. ☐



**E. Imagine you lived inside a shoe. Complete the following sentences describing your shoe-house.**

1. My shoe-house is _______________ in colour.

2. There are _______________ rooms in this house.

3. It is a _______________ house to live in.

4. The best thing about a shoe-house is _____________________________.

**F.** **The teacher will read out a story. Listen carefully and then read the sentences given below:**

*Mother was very busy. She had so many things to do. First of all, she went to the shop. There, she bought food. After that, she went to the post office to mail a letter. Next, she went to the dry cleaners to pick up a dress. Then, she went to the bank to get some money. It was now time to pick up the children from school. Finally, she went home to rest. What a busy day it was!*

**The teacher will now read out the story once again. Now, mark out whether the sentences given below are 'True' or 'False'.**

|  | TRUE | FALSE |
|---|:---:|:---:|
| First, Mom went to the shop to mail a letter. | ☐ | ☐ |
| Mom went to the dry cleaners to pick up a dress. | ☐ | ☐ |
| Mom had to go to the bank to get some money. | ☐ | ☐ |
| Mom went to the school to buy food. | ☐ | ☐ |
| Finally, Mom was free from all the work she had to do. | ☐ | ☐ |

**G.** **What these houses are called? Can you name them?**

hut        bungalow        igloo

___________   ___________   ___________

# Teacher's Note
## UNIT 1

1. **Objectives:** Listening, reading, writing and clearly inscribing letters—capital and small; making and using words and sentences; enjoying poetry; learning and reciting it; answering questions orally and in writing; applying lessons to real life; family and friends; appreciating and enjoying relationships.

2. **Listening and Speaking Skills:** Observing the world around; learning to think; right pronunciation and emphasis; learn to say words with **a** sounds.

3. **Reading and Understanding:** Read more and more passages and poems, and understand their meanings and associations; answer questions orally and in writing.

4. **Vocabulary:** Using letters correctly in words; use the right words correctly in sentences. Learn new words and meanings; people doing things for us.

5. **Grammar:** What are **sentences;** statements, questions, imperative sentences; how to write them and use them; understanding **this** and **that; these** and **those.**

6. **Writing Skills:** Neat cursive writing; using the observation and reading to write correctly.

7. **Activities:** Relate what has been learnt in the lesson to activities. Homework, etc. can be done by students on their own or with the help of their parents. Extend with more examples. For instance, the students can try to find out more about different types of homes.

8. **Values:** How we maintain good relationships with family, friends and others.

**Teacher's Role:** Examples in the book have to be used. Use examples from your own and even from the students' life. Use the blackboard. Make learning a fun journey with random questions, games, classroom competitions among the students, etc. Do not be judgemental of the children. Let them make mistakes and rectify them. The idea is to make the language attractive for them, with stories, poems and pictures. Secondly, they should start using it with some degree of confidence; There is no need for attaining perfection.

**This should be the Teacher's role and approach throughout the book.**

# 2 The Giraffe and the Monkey

**Look at the animals given below. Number them in order of height, from the shortest to the tallest:**

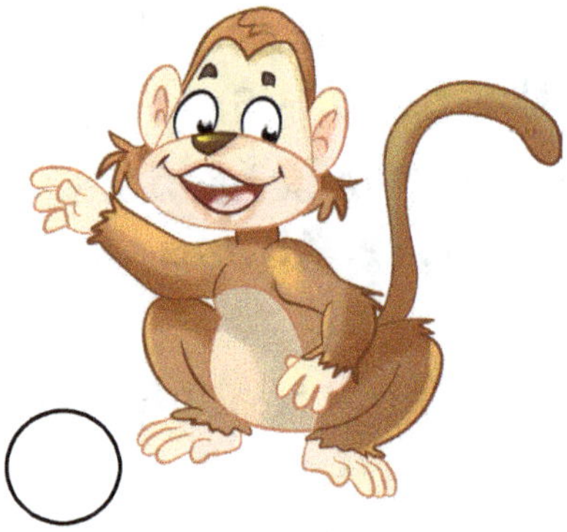

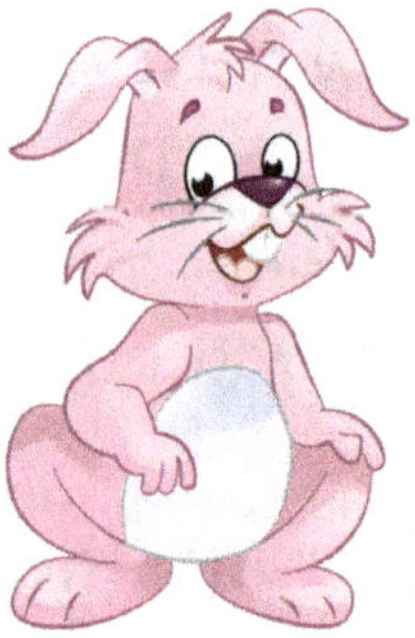

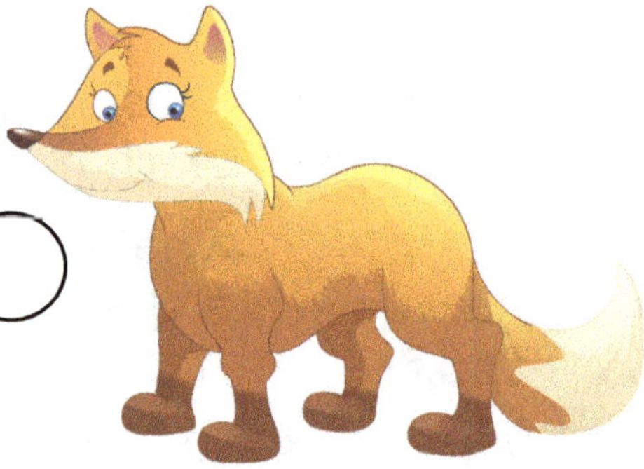

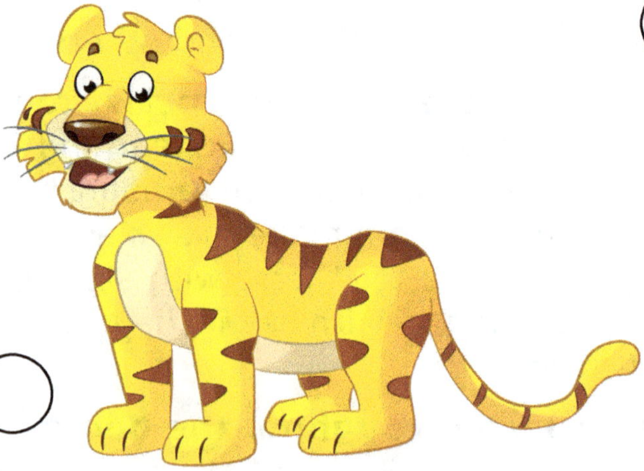

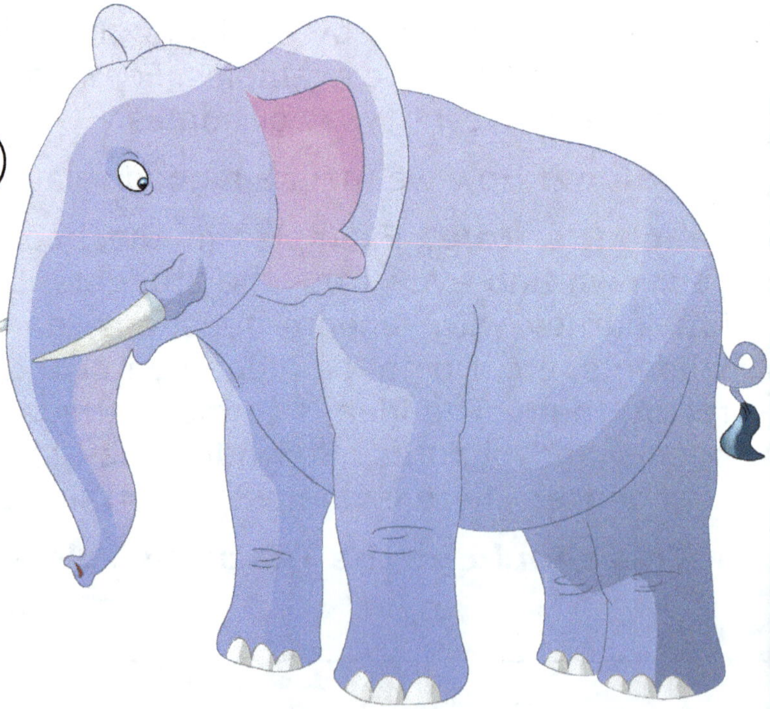

Once, there was a giraffe who lived in the forest. He was very tall. He was taller than all his brothers and sisters. He was the tallest giraffe that anyone had ever seen.

One day, the giraffe wanted to eat a fruit. It was at the top of a tall tree. It was the most delicious looking fruit. The giraffe reached out, but the fruit was too far. He could not reach it.

A small monkey saw this. He went up to the giraffe and said, "I can help you to reach the fruit."

The monkey jumped onto the giraffe's back and climbed up his neck. Then, he stretched out his long arm and plucked the fruit.

The giraffe and the monkey could not reach the fruit alone. But together, they were able to help each other.

**We should always help others.**

**A. Fill up the blanks with the right words:**

1. The _____________________ was very tall. (monkey/giraffe)

2. The fruit was at the _________________ of the tree. (top/bottom)

3. The giraffe and the monkey could not reach the fruit _________________. (alone/together)

4. We should always _________________ others. (help/not help)

**B.** **Based on the story, write whether the following statements are 'True' or 'False':**

1. The giraffe was very short.  _______________

2. The giraffe wanted to eat the fruit.  _______________

3. The monkey climbed up the giraffe's neck.  _______________

4. The fruit was at the top of the tree.  _______________

5. The monkey could not reach the fruit.  _______________

**C.** **Find the names of the following fruits from the word-grid:**

| M | O | E | G | M | J | B | I |
|---|---|---|---|---|---|---|---|
| A | P | P | L | E | G | A | U |
| N | W | X | E | L | H | N | B |
| G | R | A | P | E | S | A | X |
| O | F | N | A | C | A | N | Q |
| R | W | P | P | T | B | A | E |
| T | Q | V | U | Y | O | H | Y |
| P | A | P | A | Y | A | N | L |

Mango

Grapes

Banana

Apple

Papaya

**D.** **Look at the picture given below and complete the following sentences using the words from the box:**

monkey

trees

birds

two

tall

1. There are many green _____________________ in the forest.

2. The _____________________ is eating a banana.

3. There are _____________________ tigers near the lion.

4. The _____________________ are flying in the sky.

5. The giraffes are very _____________________.

## GRAMMAR

Naming words are called **Nouns**. They help us to name all the things around us whether they are persons, places, animals or things.

**E. Think and write two naming words for each letter:**

a: _______apple_______     _______ant_______

b: _______________     _______________

c: _______________     _______________

s: _______________     _______________

t: _______________     _______________

r: _______________     _______________

**F. Write the given naming words in the correct columns:**

| Mary   | bear    | Rohan | tiger  |
| Reena  | Matthew | bag   | Mumbai |
| France | grapes  | Delhi | London |
| horse  | book    | camel | shirt  |

| Person | Place | Animal | Thing |
| --- | --- | --- | --- |
|  |  |  |  |
|  |  |  |  |
|  |  |  |  |
|  |  |  |  |

**G.** **Your teacher will speak out the following words from the story. Repeat the words after he/she has spoken them aloud:**

1. giraffe
2. monkey
3. friend
4. stretch
5. jumped
6. together

**H.** **Let's read aloud:**

My l<u>e</u>g hurts.　　My shirt is <u>re</u>d.　　He is <u>te</u>n years old.　　We get <u>we</u>t in the rain.

Each of the underlined words has a similar sound. This is the sound of 'e'. Think of three more words that use this sound.



**I.** **Match the animal names to their pictures:**

Dog　　Cat　　Sheep　　Horse　　Duck

**J.** **Look at the pictures and compare the pairs. The first sentence has been done for you as an example.**

1. The giraffe is **taller** than Roy.

   Roy is **shorter** than the giraffe. (taller/shorter)

2. Jenny is ________________________________.

   Sam is ____________________. (darker/fairer)

3. Uncle Ben is ______________________________.

   Milly is ________________________________.

   (older/younger)



**K.** **Can you help Sammy find all the items he needs to get ready for school? Tick (✓) the things that you can arrange for him:**

comb ☐          clothes ☐

books ☐          bag ☐

shoes ☐          umbrella ☐

**L.** **Discuss in the Class:**

Could the monkey have reached the fruit without the help of the giraffe?

# Teacher's Note
## UNIT 2

1. **Objectives:** Listening, reading, writing, inscribing letters, recognising and making words; using words correctly; making sentences; understanding meanings and associations and comparison; answering questions orally and in writing; learning about animals and kindness to others; nouns.

2. **Listening and Speaking Skills:** Read aloud; learning the correct way to pronounce words, especially 'e' sounds. Learning about comparisons among things by seeing and hearing about them, and knowing what is true or false. Learn to say the words and use them.

3. **Reading and Understanding:** Associating pictures with ideas and words; Putting them into words and sentences. Understanding what a question is and how to answer it. Filling gaps in sentences; saying whether a statement is true or false. Answer questions orally and in writing.

4. **Vocabulary:** Names and houses of animals and birds; finding words on a grid, which helps to learn spelling them; what are word-meanings and their opposites – using the pictures to help as clues; naming things. Random naming games, whenever you have spare time.

5. **Grammar:** Naming things: people, animals and birds, places and things. Names of special people, places and things. Names of general people, places and things. How do we describe things and compare them? What words to use and how the words change. Make naming things into a fun game.

6. **Writing Skills:** Constant practice of letters, words and cursive writing. How to write words, gaps between words in a sentence, capital letters, full stops and question marks. The teacher should help the children to transcribe letters and words, holding their hands where necessary.

7. **Activities:** Making lists of things; this can be made into an activity with groups of five or six children. Each group can be given different lists to make. Name 5 things in the class; name 5 things at home; names of 5 places; names of 5 games we play; names of 5 classmates, etc. They can also list things they can do to help people- at home, in the class, on the road, etc.

8. **Values:** Learning that comparison should be healthy, and not for letting down people. Helping people is important. How do we help them without putting ourselves at risk? For example, fire can be dangerous. What are the safety concerns for others and for ourselves? Explain caution and courage.

# 3 The Rainbow Story

Name any four things that you can see in the picture.

1. ________________________________

2. ________________________________

3. ________________________________

4. ________________________________

Once upon a time, all the colours of the world started to fight. Each of them said that it was the best colour.

**GREEN** said, "I was chosen for grass, leaves and trees. I am the best colour."

**BLUE** said, "I am the colour of water and sky. I am the best colour."

**YELLOW** smiled and said, "I am the colour of the Sun. I am obviously the best."

**ORANGE** said, "I am the colour of health and strength. I am the best."

**RED** shouted out, "I am the brightest colour. I am the best."

**VIOLET** said, "I am the colour of power. I am the best."

Finally, **INDIGO** spoke, "I am the colour of peace. I am the best."

Suddenly, there was a startling flash of lightning! And, rain started to pour down. The colours were scared and stopped fighting.

The rain said, "You are all being silly. Don't you know that all colours are equal? You should all work together to make this world beautiful."

The colours were sorry. They said, "From now on, when it rains, we will stretch across the sky in a great bow of colours. This will remind all creatures to live together in peace."

That is why, whenever rain falls down on the earth, a rainbow appears in the sky!

**Here is a trick to remember the colours in a rainbow. Just remember the acronym - VIBGYOR!**

| V | - | Violet |
|---|---|--------|
| I | - | Indigo |
| B | - | Blue |
| G | - | Green |
| Y | - | Yellow |
| O | - | Orange |
| R | - | Red |

## A. Fill up the blanks with correct words:

1. All the colours thought that they were the most ___________.
(useful/useless)

2. ___________________ was the colour chosen for grass and trees.
(Pink/Green)

3. Blue is the colour of ___________________ and the sky.
(land/water)

4. ___________________ is the brightest colour. (Red/Blue)

5. Violet is the colour of ___________________. (power/weakness)

6. Yellow is the colour of the ___________________. (sun/moon)

7. A rainbow has ___________________ colours. (four/seven)

8. We can see a rainbow after the ___________________. (snow/rain)

9. ___________________ does not appear in the rainbow. (pink/yellow)

10. Orange is the colour of ___________________. (health/dizzness)

## B. Answer the following questions:

1. Who brought all the colours together? ___________________________ .

2. What does VIBGYOR stand for?

| | | |
|---|---|---|
| V __ O __ ET | | YE__ __ OW |
| IND __ GO | | O__ ANG__ |
| B __ UE | | R __ D |
| GR__ __ N | | |

## WORD POWER

**C.   Match the following pictures with their names:**

- Roses

- Kangaroo

- Duckling

- Carrots

## GRAMMAR

**Articles: Using 'a' and 'an'**

When a word begins with a vowel sound, we use 'an' before it. For the sound of all other letters, we use 'a' before the word. For example:

This is **a** cat.                              This is **an** egg.

**D.   Look at the pictures and fill up the blanks with a or an:**

1.   This is a book.

2.   ____________ igloo is made of ice blocks.

3.  This is _______ elephant.

4.  This is _______ house.

5.  This is ______ umbrella.

**E. Look at the pictures and complete the sentences given below. The first one has been done as an example.**

a book   a dog   an apple   an ice-cream

1. Annie is eating an apple.

2. Jimmy is reading ________________________________.

3. Dan is eating ________________________________.

4. Mary and Tim are playing with ________________________________.

**LET'S SPEAK**

**F. Your teacher will speak out the following words from the story. Repeat the words after him/her:**

1. colour
2. peace
3. rainbow
4. smile
5. health

1. Mother <u>ch</u>ecks my notebook.
2. I love to eat <u>ch</u>eese.
3. Ram sits on a <u>ch</u>air.
4. She ate her lun<u>ch</u>.

Each of the underlined words has the sound of 'ch'.
Here are some more words that use this sound.

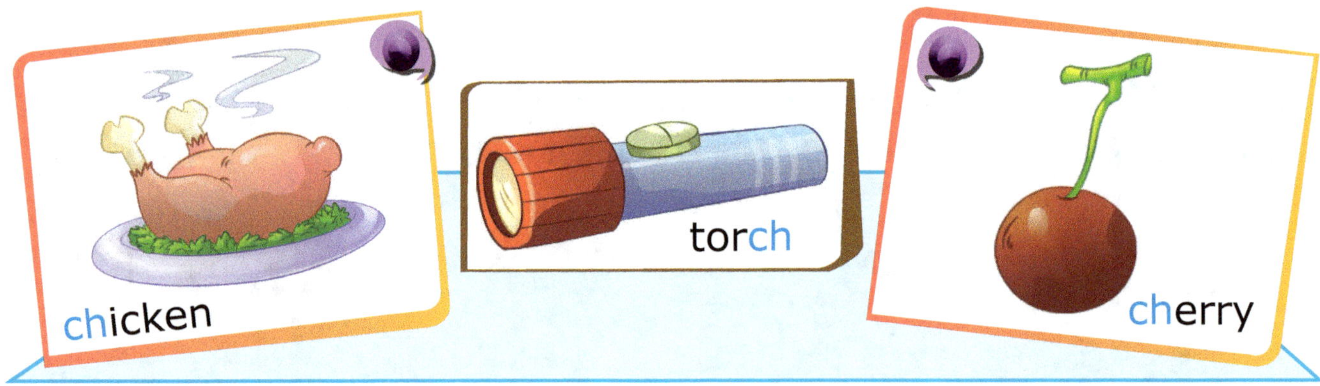

**H. Name the five objects you use in your daily life. One has been done as an example:**

1. I use a <u>comb</u> every day.

2. I use a _________________ to brush my teeth.

3. I write with a _________________.

4. I write on _________________.

5. I wear _________________.

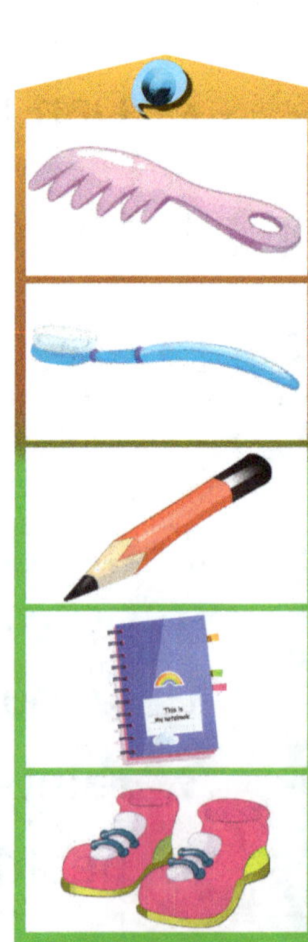

**I. Look at the pictures and complete the sentences:**

1. Sheila likes to ________________________________. 

2. Ravi goes to ________________________________. 

3. My house ________________________________. 

4. Ira's pet cat ________________________________. 

**J. Let's make a rainbow:**

Cut 7 paper strips and fill them up with the colours of rainbow using crayons. Now glue these strips together to form a rainbow. Paste cotton balls on each side to show clouds.

# Teacher's Note
## UNIT 3

1. **Objectives:** Listening, reading and writing clearly. Enjoy a prayer. Learn new words. Read a story aloud and do comprehension activities. Understand that homophones are words that sound the same but have different spellings and meanings. Write and speak a self-introduction. Study nouns.

2. **Listening and Speaking Skills:** Recitation of a prayer for family and new words related to family with correct intonation. The students can also prepare their own prayer which they would like to say with the family on the dining table.

3. **Reading and Understanding:** Read the stories and poems and answer the given questions, choose the right words, write true or false, and answer high order thinking questions. These comprehension activities can be done individually or in pairs.

4. **Vocabulary:** Understand what homophones are and make sentences with them. More homophones should be given and the students must make sentences for each one.

5. **Grammar:** Gather that nouns are naming words and identify common nouns and proper nouns. Write words in alphabetical order. The students may prepare a list of fruits, vegetables, animals, etc., and write the words in alphabetical order. The students must be able to name the important people and places around them and identify them as proper nouns.

6. **Writing Skills:** Write a self-introduction neatly and briefly and write the activities done with family.

7. **Activities:** Relate the first chapter to name the parts of the house. The students should draw a gift that they think a member of family would appreciate.

8. **Values:** How do we enjoy with our family?

**Teacher's Role:** The teacher will facilitate the students' understanding about the concept of family and the roles they play. He or she should assist the students to gain confidence in answering questions before the class. The teacher must have as many activities possible after class discussion and in pairs or groups.

# 4 The Perfect House

**Find the room:** A house has many different rooms. Can you spot the different rooms in this house and write their names?

1. _______________________________

2. _______________________________

3. _______________________________

4. _______________________________

In a forest, a stag wanted to build a house. So, he started clearing the bushes. He worked hard all day long. By evening, he was very tired. So, he went away, thinking, 'I will come back here in the morning.'

That night, a tiger passed by the same place. He too wanted to build a house. He thought, 'What a nice place! I will build my house here.'

The tiger spent the whole night clearing the area. In the morning, he was tired, and went away to sleep.

A little later, the stag came there. He was surprised to see that the whole area was cleared. So, he decided to start laying the floor of the house. After laying the floor, he went away.

Later that night, the tiger came back there. He now built the walls of the house. The next morning, the stag came there. He was surprised because the walls were ready. He quickly covered the roof with dry grass. The house was complete!

The stag was tired, so he went in and fell asleep. Late that night, the tiger, too, went into the house and fell asleep.

What do you think happened, the next morning?

Both the stag and the tiger were shocked to see each other! Both the animals ran away, leaving their perfect house empty!

**READ AND TELL**

**A.  Answer the following questions by choosing the right option:**

1.  Which two animals wanted to build a house?

    _________________________________.  (stag and tiger/tiger and lion)

2.  Which animal started clearing the bushes?

    _____________________________.  (stag/tiger)

3.  Which animal started laying the floor for the house?

    ______________________________.  (stag/rabbit)

4.  Which animal built the walls of the house?

    ______________________________.  (lion/tiger)

5.  What did the stag use to make the roof of the house?

    _________________________________.  (cement/dry grass)

6.  Why did both animals run away? _________________________________

    ____________________.  (they did not like each other/they got shocked)

**B.** **Put a Tick (✓) if the statement is 'True' and a Cross (✗) if it is 'False':**

1. The stag built the house alone. ☐

2. The tiger worked on the house during the night. ☐

3. The roof of the house was covered with bricks. ☐

4. The stag was scared to see the tiger in the house. ☐

5. The stag and the tiger were best friends. ☐

**WORD POWER**

**C.** **Use the clues to solve the crossword. Remember, it is all about houses!**

clean
shelter
bed
dining
kitchen
dog

**ACROSS**

3. We should keep our house ________________________ and tidy.

4. The room where we cook food is called the ________________________.

5. A kennel is the house of a ________________________.

6. We sleep in the ________________________ room.

**DOWN**

1. A house is also called a ________________________.

2. We eat in the ________________________ room.

**D. Read the poem and answer the following questions:**

*Thirty days has September,*
*April, June and November*
*All the rest have thirty-one,*
*Except for February alone!*

1. How many days are there in the month of May?

   a. Thirty  b. Thirty-one  c. Twenty-nine

2. Which month comes after June?

   a. April  b. August  c. July

3. Which is the first month of the year?

   a. January  b. February  c. March

4. Which of the following months has thirty days?

   a. March  b. September  c. October

## GRAMMAR

**E. Find the naming words from the given paragraph. The first sentence has been done for you:**

<u>Neel</u> went to the <u>park</u>. He played football with Shyam and Anita. Later, they had sandwiches for lunch. The park had a pond with many fish. They decided to feed their leftover bread to the fish in the pond. The fish swam to the edge to catch the bread.

## LET'S SPEAK

**F. Your teacher will speak out the following words from the story. Repeat the words after he/she has spoken them out:**

1. floor  2. roof  3. wall
4. surprise  5. perfect  6. quickly

## G. Let's read aloud:

1. The ball is behind the <u>bush</u>.
2. Mother went to the <u>shop</u>.
3. <u>Sh</u>e likes to eat fi<u>sh</u>.
4. We all sat in the <u>sh</u>ade.

Each of the underlined words has the sound of 'sh'.

**Think of three more words that have the sound of 'sh'.**

## H. Match the animal houses with their names:

nest

spider's web

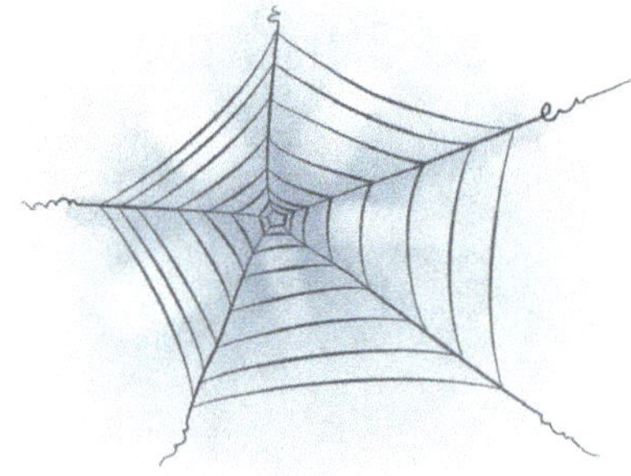

hut

kennel

## I. We all live in different houses. Can you describe your house?

1. My house has ______________ rooms.

2. ______________ people live in my house.

3. My house is made of __________________ (bricks/stones/wood) and cement.

4. My favourite room is the _______________________________.

5. I sleep in my _______________________________.

**J. Look at the picture and complete the sentences:**

big    hole in the wall    the hole    hole    scared

1. Sara's house was very ______________________.

2. One day, she saw a ______________________.

3. The mouse lived in ______________________.

4. The Sara was ______________ to see the mouse.

5. The mouse ran back into the ______________________ and did not come out again.

**K. Read the sentences given below and number the pictures according to them:**

1. Mohan goes to a library.
2. He takes a book.
3. He returns home.
4. He reads the book.

**L. Discuss in the Class:**

Do you think the stag and the tiger would have made the house so quickly on their own? What do you think they should do now?

## The Mulberry Bush

*Here we go round the Mulberry bush,*
*the Mulberry bush, the Mulberry bush,*
*Here we go round the Mulberry bush,*
*on a cold and frosty morning.*

*This is the way we wash our face,*
*wash our face, wash our face,*
*This is the way we wash our face,*
*on a cold and frosty morning.*

*This is the way we comb our hair,*
*comb our hair, comb our hair,*
*This is the way we comb our hair,*
*on a cold and frosty morning.*

*This is the way we brush our teeth,*
*brush our teeth, brush our teeth,*
*This is the way we brush our teeth,*
*on a cold and frosty morning.*

*This is the way we put on our clothes,*
*put on our clothes, put on our clothes,*
*This is the way we put on our clothes,*
*on a cold and frosty morning.*

**Have you heard this poem before? What does this poem tell us about?**

We do some activities every single day. These are called our daily routine. We all have a routine that we follow. We learn these activities from our parents and other elders in the house.

## READ AND TELL

**A.   Read the poem again and fill up the blanks with correct words:**

1.  We wake up ______________ (early/late) every morning.

2.  Then we ____________ (brush/wash) our face and ____________________

    (dirty/comb) our hair.

3.  We ________________ (wash/brush) our teeth every morning.

4.  We wear clean ____________________ (clothes/paper) after a bath.

5.  We should ______________________ (excercise/sleep) to stay fit and
    active.

## WORD POWER

**B.   Find the following words in the word-grid:**

bath   morning   sleep   brush   neat   clean   healthy

| m | o | r | n | i | n | g | f |
|---|---|---|---|---|---|---|---|
| i | z | a | s | r | e | r | h |
| b | a | t | h | y | a | e | e |
| r | b | i | l | e | t | s | a |
| u | w | q | r | g | b | c | l |
| s | l | e | e | p | k | v | t |
| h | m | b | d | e | s | e | h |
| r | c | l | e | a | n | w | y |

### One and Many

When we talk about one object or thing, we use the singular form. For example, one monkey, one boy, one table, one song.

When we talk about more than one object or thing, we use the plural form. **For example:**

**As you can see, we often add 's' to the end of a word to make it plural.**

**C.** Complete the table by writing **singular** or **plural** forms of the given words. The first one is done for you:

| Singular | Plural |
| --- | --- |
| book | books |
| ant | |
| hen | |
| | chairs |
| | goats |
| | mats |
| song | |
| apple | |
| | pens |
| bottle | |
| | trees |

**Now look at these sentences:**

a.  The hen is in the barn.
    The hens are in the barn.

b.  The book is on the table.
    The books are on the table.

c.  The boy is sleeping.
    The boys are sleeping.

d.  The girl is playing.
    The girls are playing.

e.  The monkey is sitting on the tree.
    The monkeys are sitting on the tree.

How is a sentence in each pair different from the other? The first sentence in the pair is singular; we add **'s'** to make the noun plural in the second sentence.

Have you noticed another change in the plural sentences? We use **'is'** with singular nouns and **'are'** with plural nouns.

**D.  Fill up each blank with 'is' or 'are':**

1.  The cats ________________ playing in the garden.

2.  Sohan ________________ going to school.

3.  Shyam and Ravi ________________ in the bus.

4.  Red ________________ my favourite colour.

5.  The mangoes ________________ ripe and tasty.

6.  The clock says it ________________ 8:00.

7.  Your cookies ________________ delicious.

8.  One apple ___________ red while the other ________________ green.

**E.  Look at the pictures and mark these daily activities:**

| brushing teeth | waking up | combing hair |
| --- | --- | --- |
| taking a bath | | wearing clothes |

__________________________________

__________________________________

__________________________________

__________________________________

__________________________________

# Teacher's Note
## UNIT 4

1. **Objectives:** Listening to, reading, understanding and answering different types of questions. Pronunciation of words with **sh,** words in grids. Completing sentences with words and phrases. Learning about daily routines and months, dates, numbers in words. Learning to cooperate, not being afraid. Sequencing a story in pictures. Nouns- **one and many,** and using **is** and **are** with them correctly to make sentences.

2. **Listening and Speaking Skills:** Words with **sh** begin by having short conversations, about homes, friends, etc. Read aloud to the students and let them learn the correct pronunciation. Let them learn the poems and recite them. The Mulberry Bush can be recited in groups with actions and can be sung too.

3. **Reading and Understanding:** Students can take turns reading the parts of the lesson, in groups to begin with. Comprehension: understand and answer MCQs, True/False and answers that need full sentences. Seeing a story in pictures and sequencing it.

4. **Vocabulary:** Learning the names of the homes of animals and things/rooms in your own home, observing and describing things. Words in crossword/grid. Poem of days in various months; spellings of months and days, numbers in words.

5. **Grammar:** Recognising Nouns. One and many [Singular and Plural]- how to make plurals. How to use them with **is** and **are** in order to make sentences. Explain how the noun and its number must agree to the verb used. Completing sentences using words and phrases.

6. **Writing Skills:** Writing out a to p. How to write full sentences as answers to questions. Describing things in your home, etc. See the story in pictures and orally tell the story in sequence. Then write it down neatly. Write the names of the months, the days of the week and the numbers in words from 1 to 50.

7. **Activities:** Performance poetry: The Mulberry Bush : Memorise it in groups—one group for one stanza; act out the daily activities; you can sing it too. You can have two groups in the class for Nouns: One and Many. Each group will give a word and the other will match it with its plural/singular. List out all the things you use every day. This can be done in 4 groups: getting ready; eating food; studying; playing.

8. **Values:** Setting a healthy daily routine is important. Also, it is necessary to get on well with people around us, and to cooperate with one another rather than to quarrel. Use the VIBGYOR story to explain the importance of cooperation and friendship.

# 5 Heidi's Wonderful Day

**COME ALONG**

Look at the picture given below. What do you think it shows? What do you think, the story could be about?

Choose from the options given below or think of your own:

a   A picnic

b.   A party

c.   A day in the mountains

d.   A festival

When Heidi woke up in the morning, Grandfather asked her if she wanted to go with the goats up the mountain. Heidi ran to wash her face and brush her teeth.

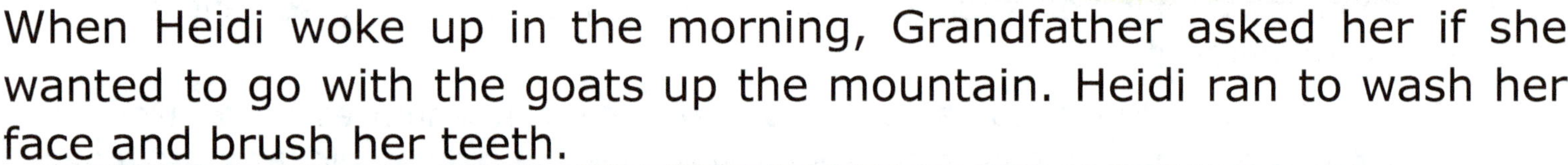

Grandfather gave Heidi some bread and cheese to eat. Peter, the goatherd, came to Grandfather's house. Soon, Peter and Heidi were climbing the mountains and running on the soft grass with the goats. Heidi had never felt so happy in her life before.

After a while, they sat down to have their bread and cheese. Heidi's loaf of bread was much larger than Peter's. She broke off some bread and gave it to him, saying, "You can have this. I have plenty."

For a minute, Peter was too surprised to speak. No one else had ever shared his food with him before. Then he happily ate it up, for he was very hungry.

When the sun started to go down over the mountain peaks, Heidi suddenly sprang to her feet. "Peter! Look, the mountains are on fire!

Look at the trees; look at the rocks! Everything is on fire!"

When she reached Grandfather's hut, Heidi told Grandfather about everything she had seen that day, especially the beautiful fire that had lit up the rocks in the evening. Heidi asked Grandfather what it was.

"When the sun says good night to the mountains, he throws his most beautiful colours over them," said Grandfather.

Heidi was very happy with this answer and went to bed dreaming of shining mountains with red roses all over them.

(Adapted from *Heidi by Johanna Spyri*)

## READ AND TELL

**A.    Tick (✓) the correct answer:**

1. Grandfather asked Heidi if she wanted to ______________

   a. go to school.

   b. go up the mountains with the goats.

2. What did Peter and Heidi do all day?

   a. They climbed mountains and ran on the soft grass.

   b. They played video games.

3. Peter was surprised when Heidi gave him more bread and cheese because __________________.

   a. he was not hungry.

   b. no one else had ever shared his food with him before.

4. Heidi went to sleep dreaming of __________________

   a. shining mountains with red roses on them.

   b. clouds and rain.

## B. Match the following:

Heidi

Peter

grandfather

goat

**WORD POWER**

## C. Read the poem and fill up the blanks with the right answers:

Butterfly, butterfly,
Colourful and bright,

Butterfly, butterfly,
So beautiful and light,

Flitting over flowers,
Red, yellow and white,

Butterfly, butterfly,
Fly as high as a kite!

1. Butterflies are ________________ . (black/colourful)

2. They ________________ over flowers. (fly/crawl)

3. Baby butterflies are called ________________ . (kittens/caterpillars)

4. Butterflies can fly very ________________. (high/badly)

5. We can often see butterflies in ________________. (summer/winter)

**D. Form new words by changing only one letter in each word. One has been done as an example.**

1. FOOD       GOOD       GOLD
2. WALL       ____ALL       BAL____
3. COLD       ____OLD       HOL____
4. MILK       MIL____       ____ILL
5. CALF       ____ALF       HAL____

## GRAMMAR

Action words are **Verbs**. They tell what subjects are doing. Look at the sentence: Mita sings.

Here, **'sings'** is the action word as it tells us *what* Mita (subject) is *doing*.

**E. Read the following sentences and write down the action words. The first one has been done for you:**

1. The boy runs.       *runs* _______________________
2. Mita colours a picture.       _______________________
3. Birds can fly.       _______________________
4. Bob sings well.       _______________________
5. Mother listens to us.       _______________________

**F. Fill up the blanks with the given action words given in the box:**

1. Sita _______________________ her hair.
2. Raman _______________________ a new book every day.
3. Shamoli _______________________ her food.
4. Jack _______________________ his face in the morning.
5. The dog _______________________ all the time.

| combs |
| eats |
| washes |
| barks |
| reads |

**G.** **Your teacher will speak out the following words from the story. Repeat the words after he/she has spoken them out:**

1. goatherd
2. mountain
3. jumping
4. grandfather
5. shining
6. hungry

**H.** **Let's read aloud:**

1. He covered the <u>roo</u>f.
2. I saw a ba<u>boo</u>n in the <u>zoo</u>.
3. A horse's <u>foo</u>t is called a <u>hoo</u>f.
4. I will see you <u>soo</u>n.

Each of the underlined words has a similar sound. This is the long vowel sound of 'oo'. Think of three more words that contain the long vowel sound of 'oo'.



**I.** **Have you ever been on a picnic? Try to remember where you went, and what you ate. Then write it down on your notebook.**

**J.** **Encircle the words that you think belong to a picnic:**

tree          sandwiches

shopping      birds

ball          doctor

tiger        book

games       frisbee

friends      table

**K. Use the following words and make sentences of your own:**

1. mountain - ______________________________________

2. hungry - ______________________________________

3. dream - ______________________________________

4. plenty - ______________________________________

**L. Use the rhyming words from the box below and create a new poem:**

sight    me    sky

Far away and up so high,
The sun shines brightly in the ________________.

In the garden, under the tree
The warm sunrays fall on ________________.

The sun makes everything so bright
I will never forget this lovely ________________.

**M. Can you think of two more rhyming words for each of the following?**

1. sing   ________________        ________________

2. late   ________________        ________________

3. moon   ________________        ________________



**N. Why did Heidi think the mountains were on fire? Have you ever seen such a sight?**

# Teacher's Note
## UNIT 5

1. **Objectives:** Listening, speaking, reading, writing. Answering MCQs. Associating words with pictures and other words. Pronounce words with **oo.** Make your own sentences. Poetry: recitation, answers and rhyming words. Word formation. Verbs – action words and their usage. The pleasure of enjoying Nature and of sharing.

2. **Listening and Speaking Skills:** Read aloud. Students can follow. Say words correctly for them to learn pronunciation. Words with **oo** can be highlighted. Let them learn and recite the poems.

3. **Reading and Understanding:** After you have read the story once, ask random students to read a sentence, at a time. Ask them MCQs orally; then mark the answers in the books. Make sentences with words orally, so that it becomes a game. Read poetry and explain.

4. **Vocabulary:** Draw attention to new words and their meanings. Show them the association of words with pictures, objects and other words, using examples in the book and in the class. How to change words by changing a letter at a time. Explain rhyming words and find them.

5. **Grammar:** What are Verbs – Action words? Make the students suggest more action words. Start conversations using the words. Do the exercises orally and then write them.

6. **Writing Skills:** Write q to z. Make sentences with the words given. Do this orally with any words that the students like. Two groups can be formed. One group suggests a word; the other group makes a sentence. Do this alternately. Then write it on the board. They can transcribe a few. Cursive writing practice to continue.

7. **Activities:** Word and sentence games as mentioned above should become a daily routine. Try word building too, with one child giving a letter at a time. The teacher writes it on the board. For example: I, IN, INK, INTO, INDIA, etc.

8. **Values:** Draw attention to the story. It highlights two things: (i) sharing things with friends; and (ii) enjoying the beauty of Nature, like sunset on the mountains. Relate to daily life: sharing notes, homework, lunch, etc.; enjoying playing in the park, seeing the flowers, trees, sunrise, animals and birds, etc. around us.

## Read the passage and answer the following questions:

Mohit wants to build a birdhouse. He gets some wood. He gets some nails and paint. His dad helps too. He gets a saw and a hammer. He also gets a pencil and a ruler. Mohit draws his birdhouse. They build it together. Then, they hang it up in a tree. A bird goes into the birdhouse.

**A. Answer each question to complete the sentence:**

1. What does Mohit wants to build?

   Mohit wants to build a ______________.

2. Who helps Mohit?

   Mohit's ______________ helps him.

3. Where do they put the birdhouse?

   They hang it up in a ______________.

**B. Write the colour of each of these:**

1. ______________ sky
2. ______________ mountain
3. ______________ sunflower
4. ______________ grass
5. ______________ water
6. ______________ rose

**C. Fill up each blank with 'a' and 'an' to complete the sentence:**

1. I saw ________ eagle sitting on my terrace.
2. ________ aeroplane was flying high in the sky.
3. Can you tell me ________ story?
4. I will finish work in ________ hour.
5. It is ________ hot day.
6. Alex is ________ honest boy.

**D. Read the names in each group and classify them as names of persons, places, animals or things:**

| Chair | Table | Pencil | Notebook | Dog | Cat |
| Sparrow | Lion | Temple | City | Raman | |
| Village | Mohit | Hedit | Mona | Postoffice | |

| Person | Place | Animal | Thing |
| --- | --- | --- | --- |
|  |  |  |  |
|  |  |  |  |
|  |  |  |  |
|  |  |  |  |

**E.  Encircle the odd word in each group:**

1  frog            turtle            sparrow
2. eagle           pigeon            tree
3. chocolate       chair             table

**F.  Complete the follwing grid with double-letter words:**

| | | | | | | | | | | |
| --- | --- | --- | --- | --- | --- | --- | --- | --- | --- | --- |
| 1. | b | u |   |   | e | r | f | l | y | |
| 2. | c | h |   |   | s | e | | | | |
| 3. | s | h |   |   | p | | | | | |
| 4. | u | m | b | r | e |   |   | a | | |
| 5. | k | i |   |   | e | n | | | | |

**G.  Complete the sentences by using the verbs from the box:**

> **writes        eat        walk**

1. I ______________ an apple every day.

2. Tim ______________ letters to his cousin.

3. We ______________ on the pavement.

**H.  Fill up each blank using 'is' or 'are':**

1. This ________ my book.            3. These ________ flowers.

2. We ________ studying.            4. She ________ reading a book.

**I.  Answer these questions from the lessons you have read:**

1. Who lived in the shoe?

_______________________________________________

2. Who was Heidi's friend?

_______________________________________________

# 6 The Raven and the Fox

Each one of us is good at something. This is our **talent**.

Sara is a good singer.

Pete can run very fast.

Emma draws very well.

What is your special talent?_________________________________________

**We should always be humble. This means we should not become proud of our talent.**

One day, Mr. Raven was sitting on the branch of a tree. He was black in colour but very good-looking. He was also very vain.

Rick, the Fox came and sat under the same tree. He looked up and saw Mr. Raven who had a slice of bread in his beak. Rick was hungry. His stomach rumbled. He wanted to eat the bread.

He thought for a while and then he came up with a good idea.

"Mr. Raven, you are so handsome," said Rick, "Your feathers are so shiny and long. If you could sing well, you would be the king of the birds."

Mr. Raven was very happy to hear the lovely words. He thought, 'At last, someone has realised how wonderful and talented I am!'

He was so proud that he forgot he could not sing. He wanted to show the Fox that he could sing well. He opened his beak to sing, and the slice of bread fell down to the ground.

Rick ate the bread quickly. After he had eaten the bread, he told Mr. Raven, "You are so vain. You were so flattered that you forgot all about the bread. Your loss is my gain, and I thank you for the bread."

Saying this, Rick went away. Mr. Raven felt very foolish and thought, 'I will never be so vain again!'

## READ AND TELL

**A.  Tick (✓) the right answer:**

1. The _________________ was sitting on the tree.
   a. Raven
   b. Fox

2. The Raven was ______________ in colour.
   a. blue
   b. black

3. The Fox was very _______________.
   a. hungry
   b. thirsty

4. The Fox asked the Raven to __________________.
   a. laugh
   b. sing

5. What happened as soon as the Raven opened his mouth?
   a. The Fox ran away.
   b. The bread fell down and the Fox ate it.

**B.** **Read the sentence and write 'True' or 'False':**

1. The Fox was hungry.  _______________

2. The Raven was a very good singer.  _______________

3. The Raven was very good-looking.  _______________

4. The Fox was very proud of his voice.  _______________

5. The Raven lost the bread because of his pride.  _______________

**C.** **Match the animal names with their young ones:**

dog          cat          kangaroo          horse          cow

**Now, write the names of the young ones of these animals to complete the sentences:**

1. A young dog is called a _________________________________________.

2. A young cat is called a _________________________________________.

3. A young kangaroo is called a _________________________________.

4. A young horse is called a ______________________________________.

5. A young cow is called a _________________________________________.

**D.** **Look at the pictures and answer the questions using the action words given in the box:**

jumping     sleeping     playing     eating

1. What is Rohit doing?

_______________________________________.

2. What is Bina doing?

_______________________________________.

3. What is Veena doing?

_______________________________________.

4. What is Shiv doing?

_______________________________________.

**E.** **Your teacher will speak out the following words from the story. Repeat the words after him/her:**

1. vain
2. beak
3. hungry
4. handsome
5. lovely
6. talented

**F.** **Let's read aloud:**

1. The <u>sh**ee**t</u> is dirty.
2. We brush our <u>t**ee**th</u> every day.
3. I <u>s**ee**</u> a rainbow.
4. There are <u>thr**ee**</u> girls in the class.

Each of the underlined words has a similar sound. This is the long vowel sound of 'ee'. Think of three more words that use the long vowel sound of 'ee'.



**G.** **Fill up the blanks using the sound-words from the box:**

| splash | pitter-patter | clip-clop | croak |
|---|---|---|---|

1. She heard the _______________ (sound of raindrops) on the roof.

2. Ben jumped into the puddle with a big _______________ .

3. The _______________ of frogs could be heard loud and clear from the pond.

4. The _______________ of a horse's hoofs woke him up.

 **Words those have same meaning as another one called synonyms. Match the given words to their synonyms:**

| | |
|---|---|
| vain | nice |
| above | under |
| lovely | proud |
| sad | over |
| below | upset |

**I.** **Did you read the story of the thirsty crow? Look at the pictures given below and complete the story. The first one has been done for you.**

> drinking the water    drink water    into the pot

1. The crow is thirsty and

   it is looking for water._________________.

2. The crow is trying to

   ________________________________.

3. The crow is dropping pebbles

   ________________________________.

4. The crow is

   ________________________________.

**J.** **Which animal or bird do you think is the most beautiful? Paste its picture below and write why you find it attractive?**

**K.** **Discuss in the Class:**

What is the meaning of 'vain'? What do you think you would have done if you had been the Raven? Draw and colour the picture of the vain Raven.

# Teacher's Note
## UNIT 6

1. **Objectives:** Listening, speaking, reading, writing; Answers: MCQs, gap-fill, True/False. Learning words-meanings. Noticing sounds around us. Words with **ee.** Learning more action words using +ing. Writing a picture story. Names of animals and their young ones. Recognising and speaking about talents— appreciating oneself and others. Humility v/s Vanity.

2. **Listening and Speaking Skills:** Read aloud and students repeat. Teach the right pronunciation of words. Do the exercises orally first so that the students may become confident about speaking in English. Notice all sounds present around: fan, horn, wind, bird, etc. Saying words with **ee** sounds.

3. **Reading and Understanding:** Read aloud. Ask students at random to read words or sentences. Familiarise them with seeing the words. Explain the story; then orally do the exercises: MCQs, gap-fill and True/False. Let students mark/ write each exercise as you do it with them.

4. **Vocabulary:** Learn new words: talent, vain, etc. Learn words with **ee** in spelling. Can tell them words with the sound too; like piece, peace, peas, etc. Use words to describe pictures. Encourage students to look for new words and words that describe sounds and the names of animals and their young ones.

5. **Grammar:** More about action words—Verbs. Use examples from the book and from life. Use of verb+ing in showing the action should be explained. Tell them to add am/is/are. Do the examples orally and on the blackboard. Get the pictures of actions. Use comic books/cartoons. Involve students.

6. **Writing Skills:** Write numbers 51 to 100 in words. Write a story in pictures, using given phrases. Sequencing the story line. Continue cursive writing. Make sentences with words. Do this orally, then write the sentences on the board. Students can transcribe one or two sentences.

7. **Activities:** (i) Have fun with noises and sounds of different things, even the screech of chalk on the board. (ii) Ask students to share what they, the members of their family are good at and how they do it. Some students have a talent for doing very ordinary things, so make sure that too is appreciated. Can have a Talent Chart in the class.

8. **Values:** (i) Appreciating talent in oneself without being vain, and talent in others without feeling small is important. Share stories. (ii) Why it is necessary to be humble? Conduct fun sessions in the class to explain stories like The Emperor's New Clothes, to make students understand what flattery, humility, real appreciation, etc. is.

# 7 Everyone is Important

Can you name these places?

______________________________

______________________________

______________________________

______________________________

A tree grew alone in a desert. The sun burned its bark and the hot sand covered its leaves. No other plants grew near by. But the tree kept on growing.

Every year, the tree grew taller and stronger.

It always thought, 'I am growing in the desert for a reason.'

One day, a hawk flew over the desert. He saw the tree and sat on its branch. He looked around the desert and said, "Oh, you poor tree! Why do you live alone on this hot sand? Who needs you here?"

"You," answered the tree.

"I? I don't need you," said the hawk, surprised.

"If I were not here," said the tree, "you would sit on the hot sand instead of my branch. You would have no shade from the hot sun either."

The hawk realised that the tree was right. A tree in a desert is as important as a tree in a forest.

Everyone and everything on the Earth is important.

**A. Choose the correct answer and complete the sentences:**

1. The tree grew in the ___________________________.        (forest/desert)

2. The leaves of the tree were covered with _________________________.
(sand/dewdrops)

3. One day, a ___________________ sat on the tree's branch.
(pigeon/hawk)

4. The hawk thought that ___________________ needed the tree.
(no one/the desert)

**B. Think and tell the right answer:**

1. Where did the tree grow?
The tree grew in a _________________________________________.

2. Why was the tree lonely?
The tree was lonely because _____________________________________.

3. Which bird came to sit on the tree's branch?
_________________________________________ on the tree's branch.

4. How did the tree help the hawk?
The tree helped the hawk by giving _________________________________.



**C. Words those have different meanings to each other are called opposites. Match the following words with their opposites:**

| | |
|---|---|
| rich | loose |
| sad | dark |
| weak | happy |
| tight | poor |
| bright | strong |

## D. Fill up the blanks using the correct opposites:

1. The tea is __________ but ice cream is __________
   (hot/cold)

2. The man was __________ but the boy was __________.
   (short/tall)

3. Grandmother is __________ but I am __________.
   (young/old)

4. We should sleep __________ so that we may not get up __________
   in the morning. (late/early)

5. The tree was __________ but the hawk was __________ .
   (wise/foolish)

### GRAMMAR

**Prepositions**

**Prepositions** tell us where things are. These are position words.

**For example:** The dog sits 'on' the floor. Here, 'on' is a preposition or position word. It tells us the position of the dog.

The words **on, in, under, over, near, into, up** and **around** are all prepositions.

## E. Fill up the blanks with the correct prepositions:

1. The bird is ______________ (in/under) the cage.

2. The elephant is ______________ (near/on) the drum.

3. The pencil is _____________ (under/over) the eraser.

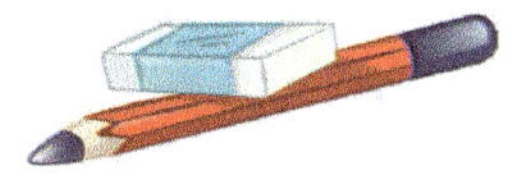

4. The dog is _____________ (near/under) the table.

5. The coat is _____________ (around/in) the cupboard.

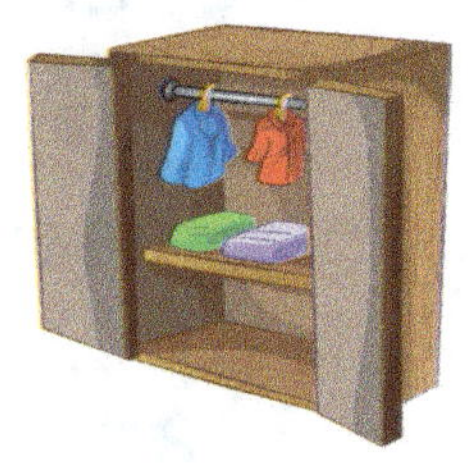

**F.** **Look at each picture and encircle the correct preposition:**

1. The eggs are in / on / under the basket.

2. The cup is in / on / under the table.

3. Mother is in / on / over the house.

4. The boy is in / on / over the can.

5. The bucket is in / under / on the well.

**G.** **Your teacher will speak out the following words from the story. Repeat the words after him/her:**

1. hawk
2. desert
3. sand
4. leaves
5. branches
6. important

**H.** **Read and study the following conversation and try it with your classmates:**

When we start a conversation, we should greet each other. Here are some common greetings that you can use:

"Hello"

"Good morning"

"Good afternoon"

"How are you?"

"Nice to meet you"

Now, start a conversation about your favourite person. You can use the hints given below.

- Who is your favourite person? (mother/father/friend, etc.)

- What do you do together? (talk, play, read, etc.)



**I.** **Fill in the blanks to complete the names of the trees:**

| oak   pine   banyan   bamboo   palm   neem |

1. b a ___ y ___n

2. oa___

3. ___in ___

4. ba ___b___o

5. pa___m

6. ___ee___

**J.    Match the given parts of a tree with their names:**

trunk

branches

roots

leaf

**K.    Choose the correct option from the bracket and rewrite the sentences:**

1. The bird (sits/grows) on the tree.

   _______________________________________________________________.

2. The tree (grows/runs) in the park.

   _______________________________________________________________.

3. The dog (barks/runs) loudly.

   _______________________________________________________________.

4. The cat (sings/sleeps) on the sidewalk.

   _______________________________________________________________.

5. The children (play/study) in the park.

   _______________________________________________________________.

**L.** **Work your way from the roots to the branch of the tree to find an apple.**

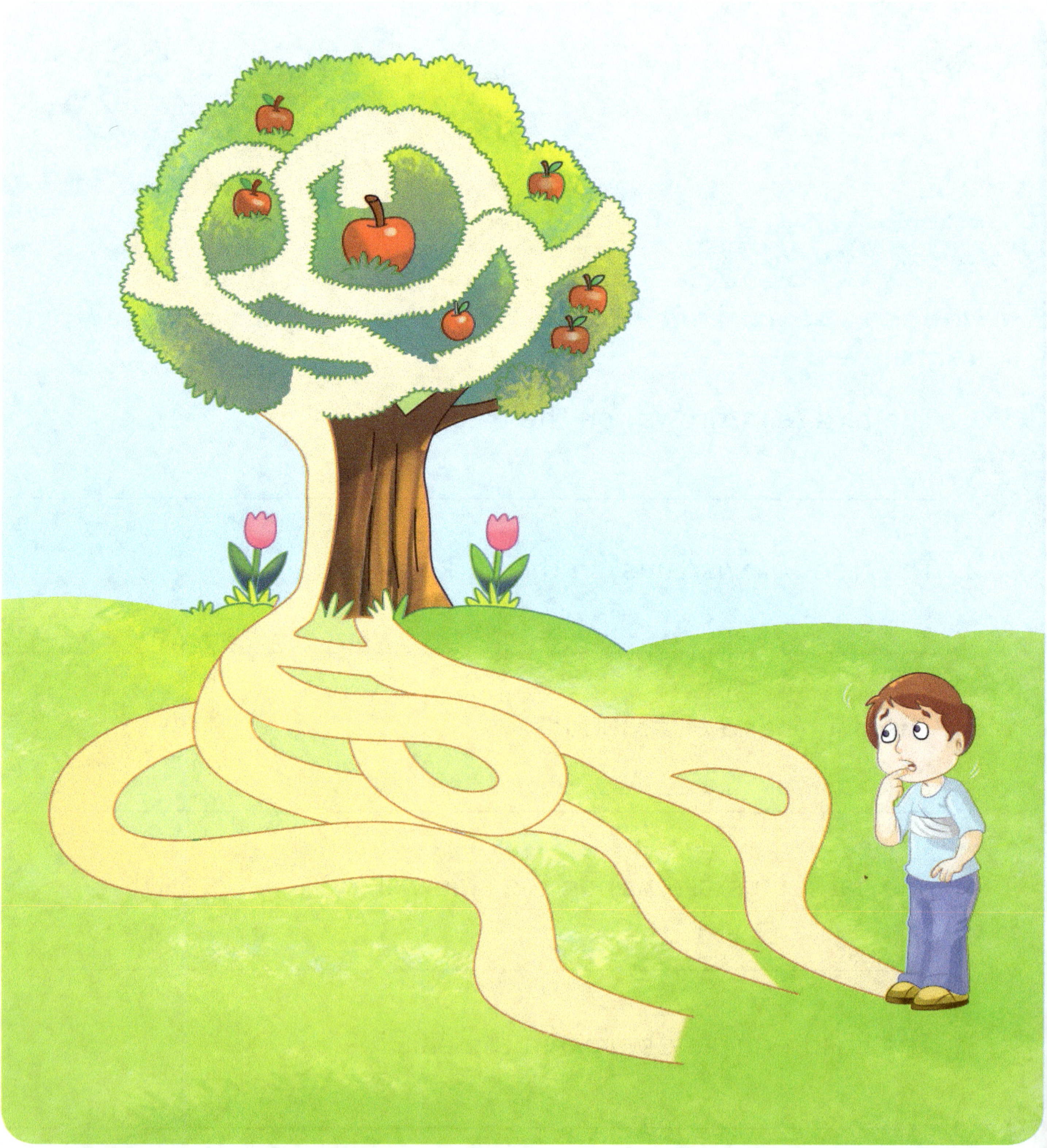

# Poem

## Ice-Cream Man

When summer's in the city,
    And the brick's a blaze of heat,
        The Ice-cream Man with his little cart
            Goes trundling down the street.

        Beneath his round umbrella,
            Oh, what a joyful sight,
                To see him fill the cones with mounds
                    Of cooling brown and white:

Vanilla, chocolate, strawberry,
    Or chilly things to drink
        From bottles full of frosty-fizz,
            Green, orange, white, or pink.

        His cart might be a flower bed,
            Of roses and sweet peas,
                The way the children cluster round
                    As thick as honeybees.

- Rachel Field

**A.** **Fill in the blanks with appropriate words:**

1. It is the ___________________ season in the city.

2. The ice-cream man carries ice creams in a ___________________ .

3. He fills ice cream in a ___________________ .

4. The children gather around him like ___________________ .

**B.** **Can you find out the rhyming words from the poem? One has been done for you as an example:**

1. heat　　:　street

2. might　:　___________________

3. drink　　:　___________________

4. peas　　:　___________________

5. hounds　:　___________________

**C.** **Selling ice creams is the ice-cream man's profession. What would you like to be when you grow up? You can take a clue from the pictures given below:**

## LET'S WRITE

### D. Compound Words:

A compound word is created when we join two different words. For example, we get *popcorn* by joining **pop** and **corn**.

pop + corn = popcorn

Remember, the new word should also have a meaning.

**Look at the two columns given below. Join the words from the two columns to make the compound words:**

| Column A | Column B | Compound Word |
|---|---|---|
| news | paper | |
| down | stairs | |
| arm | chair | |
| earth | quake | |
| air | port | |
| rain | coat | |
| note | book | |
| black | board | |
| police | man | |

### E. Identify the compound words and colour them blue:

| airport | bag | table | daytime | mail | time |
|---|---|---|---|---|---|
| hand | bookcase | call | haircut | earthquake | man |
| wheelchair | earphone | handbag | band | fish | fireplace |
| ice | hand | key | houseboat | house | lady |
| gateway | shelf | land | fire | notebook | cat |

# Teacher's Note
## UNIT 7

1. **Objectives:** Appreciate the significance of things on the earth. Listen, speak, read, understand. Answer Questions, gap-fill. Naming trees and parts of a tree. How to converse by greeting people and saying a few polite words at the beginning of a conversation. Building sentences with words and phrases. Learning about opposites, compound words. Prepositions and their usage. Poem—The Ice-Cream Man—Recitation. Understand it and answer questions; rhymes.

2. **Listening and Speaking Skills:** Read aloud; ask students to read words/sentences, pronouncing words correctly. How to converse. What do we say to greet people? Introductory conversation. Have one session on what the students want to be when they grow up. The teacher will be a Moderator, not a Judge!

3. **Reading and Understanding:** Read aloud. Ask students to read also. Explain the lesson. Explain why each thing on the earth is important: trees, grass, flowers, clouds, water, etc. Answer questions orally; then get students to write them in their books. Encourage the students to ask questions too. Try to get them to put the questions in English. It will help them converse.

4. **Vocabulary:** Do oral word and sentence-building games. What are opposites? Find opposites. Compound words. Find words that rhyme. What are the names of trees and the names of their parts. Draw on the board too or use a chart.

5. **Grammar:** What are Prepositions and how to use them. How to make correct sentences. What are compound words.

6. **Writing Skills:** Make sentences. How to build sentences using words and phrases. Do this orally first; then write it down. Continue to practise cursive writing.

7. **Activities:** Learning about: (i) Tree parts – can work with a drawing by the children or make a chart. (ii) Things on the earth – why they are significant. Collect one picture from each child and make a collage for the classroom. (iii) What is a Maze? Have fun with it.

8. **Values:** (i) Treat the earth properly. It gives us so much. (ii) Talk about what the students wish to be when they are older. Give their ambitions a healthy atmosphere to grow in. They will learn the value of a worthwhile ambition. Let them learn to appreciate also the efforts of their parents and others. This also becomes a good time to tell them how studying can help them.

# 8 A Day in the Park

We often spend time with our family and friends by doing several activities together. Look at the pictures below. Fill up the blanks with the activities children love to do with their families and friends.

1.  Simi and her brother love to

    ___________________________ together.

2.  Harry, Phil and their friends love to

    ___________________________.

3.  Ryan loves to ___________________________

    with his grandfather.

4.  Ben and Sue love to ___________________________

    with their parents.

It was a beautiful Sunday morning. Tina was playing with her doll when her brother, Fred, said, "Let us have a picnic today." Tina's father agreed to the idea. Tina's mother went into the kitchen to pack some food for the picnic. She took the basket and put food and paper plates in it.

Tina's father took out his car and put the basket of food and a large mat into the car. Soon, they reached the park. Fred took the mat and spread it on the green grass. They all sat on the mat and shared interesting stories.

Tina's mother opened the basket of food. She gave each of them a paper plate, and some sandwiches and salad. In the end, she gave them apples to munch on.

Once everyone finished eating, Tina's father carefully collected all the paper plates and asked Tina to throw them into the dustbin which was kept at the far corner of the park. Tina asked her father, "Why can't we leave the plates here?"

Father replied, "We must not dirty the beautiful park. If we keep the place clean, we will have more space to play."

After that, they started playing 'tag'. Fred ran very fast and no one was able to beat him in the game. Finally, the sun started to go down slowly. It was evening, and the stars began to come out. So, they went back home.

"This was the best day of my life!" said Tina.

## READ AND TELL

**A. Fill in the blanks with appropriate words:**

1. Tina's family drove in a ___________________ to the park.

2. They ate food in ___________________ plates.

3. Mother gave them ___________________ to munch on afterwards.

4. Fred ___________________ very fast while playing 'tag'.

5. They shared ___________________ while sitting on the mat.

6. In the evening, the ___________________ began to come out.

7. Tina was playing with her ___________________ .

8. The sun started to ___________________ slowly.

**B.   Answer the following questions:**

1.  Where did Tina and her family go to spend the day?

   _______________________________________________

2.  What did they eat for lunch?

   _______________________________________________

3.  When did stars begin to come out?

   _______________________________________________

4.  Where did they throw the paper plates?

   _______________________________________________

5.  What did they play?

   _______________________________________________

**WORD POWER**

**C.   Find all the hidden words in the word-grid:**

fruit    shade    wood    air    food    paper    nuts

| f | o | o | d | d | t | e |
|---|---|---|---|---|---|---|
| r | t | p | a | p | e | r |
| u | v | n | b | c | w | g |
| i | r | u | u | j | o | s |
| t | a | t | p | l | o | w |
| e | i | s | h | a | d | e |
| a | r | t | i | j | h | d |

The word that describes a noun is called an **Adjective** or a describing word. For example: Sheila is a **pretty** girl.

Here, **pretty** is used for describing how Sheila looks like.

**D.** **Look at the picture of the lady and fill up the blanks using the correct adjectives:**

1. Here is a ________________________ lady.          (tall/short)

2. The lady has a ____________________ face.          (pretty/plain)

3. The lady has ________________________ hair.          (long/short)

4. The lady is wearing a ____________________________ dress.     (clean/dirty)

5. The lady wears ____________________________ shoes.          (black/brown)

**E.** **Encircle the adjectives for the words given below:**

1. Hair    :    long, short, sad, old, curly

2. House    :    big, boring, small, old,
                 young, clean

3. Girl    :    sad, happy, pretty, cold,
                 hungry

4. Tree    :    pretty, tall, leafy, happy, curly

5. Tea    :    hot, tasty, angry, tight, old

**F.** **Your teacher will speak out the following words from the story. Repeat the words after him/her:**

1. picnic
2. basket
3. sandwich
4. stories
5. stars
6. collect
7. plates
8. apples

**G.** **Fill in the blanks with the names of the days of the week:**

1. The first day of the week is __________________.

   (Sunday/Saturday)

2. There are ______________ days in a week.        (seven/eight)

3. The day after Wednesday is __________________.

   (Friday/Thursday)

4. __________________ is the third day of the week. (Tuesday/Friday)

5. We go to school on __________________.        (Sunday/Monday)

**H.** **Write a letter to your cousin about your trip to the zoo by filling up the blanks with correct words:**

Dear __________________,

Hope you are well and enjoying life. I went to the _______________ (*zoo/park*) yesterday, with my friends. There, we saw a huge _______________ _______________________________ (*elephant/pineapple*) with a big trunk.

Beside it was a giraffe with a long _______________ (*neck/ear*).

The giraffe was eating _______________ (*leaves/chocolate*) from tall tree. We also saw colourful _______________ (*stones/birds*) in a big cage.

The birds were tweeting sweetly. We ate _________________________________ (*sandwiches/ice cream*) for lunch at the canteen there. We returned home in the _______________ (*evening/night/afternoon*). It was the _______________ (*best/worst*) day of my life!

Your loving cousin,

_______________________________



**ACTIVITY**

I.  **Paste a picture of your family in the box and write few lines in your notebook.**

# Teacher's Note
## UNIT 8

1. **Objectives:** Listening, speaking, reading, understanding. Punctuation. Enjoying doing things, family outing, such as going to a park/picnic. Importance of a clean environment. Answer questions, fill up gaps, Days of week. Using words to write a letter. Word grid, Learning about Adjectives-describing words and using them. Making sentences with three- letter words.

2. **Listening and Speaking:** Read aloud and keep punctuation marks in mind while reading. Discuss family outings at weekends and holidays. Going to a park or for a picnic, etc.

3. **Reading and Understanding:** Read aloud and ask the students to read after you. Explain the lesson, new words and ideas. Then do the exercises for gapfill and answering questions orally first. After that, get them to write it in their books. Pictures and real life may be related to the ideas.

4. **Vocabulary:** Days of the week, spellings, correct pronunciation, especially 'Wednesday'. Words in a grid – find them. Orally use three-letter words in small sentences.

5. **Grammar:** What are Adjectives – describing words? How are they used? Make two groups in the class–one for Nouns and one for Adjectives. One group gives a word, and the other comes up with a matching adjective. Reverse groups.

6. **Writing Skills:** Cursive writing should be continuously practised as a child is a little being for whom holding a pencil and tracing letters is an unfamiliar skill. Try making letters using plasticine/card cut-outs, etc. or crayons on a chart paper. Write small sentences, and students can also write on the blackboard one at a time.

7. **Activities:** (i) Make a Happy Day chart: what do they enjoy doing? Add sentences to it. (ii) A clean environment collage can be made. (iii) Describe Papa/Mummy/sibling/friend.

8. **Values:** (i) The importance of relaxation, and playing should be discussed. Ask them what they do with their families. (ii) How do they clean up their homes, bags, etc.? What do their parents and friends do? Why is it necessary to keep things clean and to do activities that help to relax?

# 

# The Honest Woodcutter

**COME ALONG**

### Find out and write:

- What does a woodcutter do?

  ______________________________________________________

- Look at the pictures and encircle the tool that a woodcutter uses.

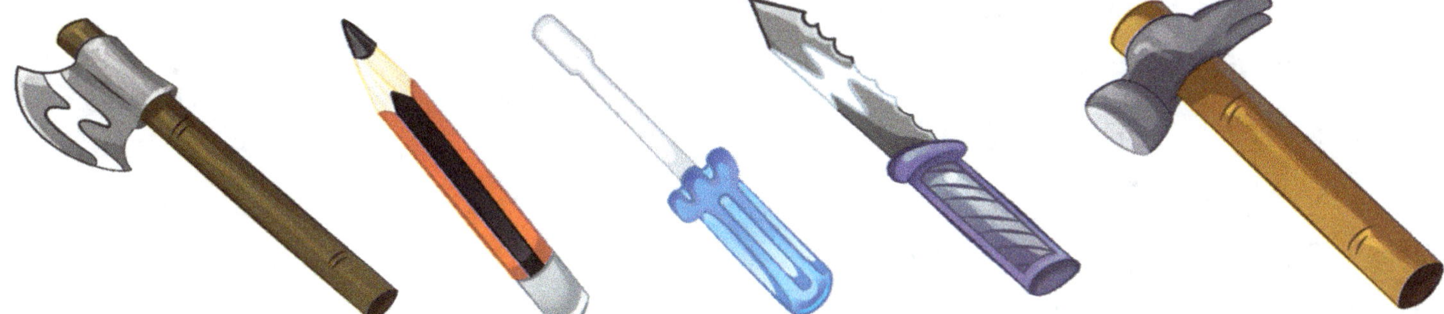

Name three things that are made up of wood.

1. ____________________  2. ____________________  3. ____________________

A poor woodcutter lived in a village near the forest. He went into the forest every day to cut wood. He sold this wood in the market and bought himself some food.

One day, while he was cutting wood, something strange happened. His axe slipped from his hand and fell into the nearby river. The river was deep and he could not see his axe anywhere. The woodcutter was sad, as he had no money to buy another axe.

Just then, a fairy appeared from the river. In her hand, she held a golden axe. She offered it to him and said, "I found this gold axe in the river. Is this yours?"

"That's not mine," replied the woodcutter.

The fairy then brought out a silver axe and asked him the same question. The woodcutter refused to take the silver axe as well. Finally, the fairy held out an iron axe.

Smiling with eyes wide open, the woodcutter said, "That's mine. Thank you very much."

The fairy was very happy with the woodcutter's honesty and said, "Such honesty deserves a reward." She gave the poor man all the three axes and disappeared. The woodcutter was no longer poor, but he always remained honest.

## A. Choose the correct answer:

1. Why was the woodcutter upset?
   a. Because he did not have money to buy food.
   b. Because he did not have money to buy a new axe.
   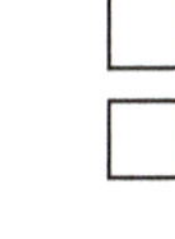

2. Why was the fairy happy with the woodcutter?
   a. Because the woodcutter was very honest.
   b. Because the woodcutter had dropped his axe into the river.

3. How many kinds of axes did the fairy offer the woodcutter?
   a. Five kinds of axes.
   b. Three kinds of axes.

## B. Fill in the blanks with correct options:

1. The woodcutter accidentally dropped his ___________ (axe/knife) into a river.

2. The woodcutter refused to take the ___________ (iron/golden) and silver axes given by the fairy.

3. The fairy was ___________ (upset/happy) with the woodcutter.

4. The woodcutter was ___________ (honest/greedy).

## C. Answer the following questions:

1. Where did the woodcutter live?

   ___________________________________________________

2. Who appeared in front of the woodcutter?

   ___________________________________________________

3. What did the fairy give to the woodcutter as a reward?

   ___________________________________________________

**D.** **Encircle the word that has the same meaning as the word given in bold:**

1. **work** : job     labour     sleep
2. **right** : correct     knot     yes
3. **talk** : laugh     that     speak
4. **forest** : jungle     wood     food

**E.** **Fill up the boxes with the missing letters:**

1. Makes furniture out of wood:    C A □ □ E N T □ R
2. Makes us laugh:    J □ K E □
3. Repairs pipes and taps:    P □ U M □ E R

When we want to write about something that is still happening, we add **'ing'** to an action word.

**For example:** eat + ing = eating      draw + ing = drawing
jump + ing = jumping      sleep + ing = sleeping

**F.** **Use 'ing' form of the verbs to complete the sentences:**

1. Shyamoli is _______________ (sing) in the competitio
2. Ron is _______________ (call) Tim on the phone.
3. Lily is _______________ (sleep).
4. Mother is _______________ (cook) in the kitchen.
5. The teacher is _______________ (talk) to the students
6. Marie is _______________ (play) in the park.
7. Ryan is _______________ (eat) a burger.

**G. Change the following by adding 'ing' to them:**

1.  sleep  ___________________________
2.  cry  ___________________________
3.  try  ___________________________
4.  fall  ___________________________
5.  lick  ___________________________
6.  wear  ___________________________



**H.  Your teacher will speak out the following words from the story. Repeat the words after him/her:**

1.  axe
2.  woodcutter
3.  honest
4.  reward
5.  river
6.  refuse

**I.  Have the below conversation with your classmates and fill up the blanks:**

1.  Where do you live?

    I live in ____________.

2.  What do you like to do?

    I like to ____________. (play/draw/sing)

3.  What do you want to be when you grow up?

    I want to be a ____________. (pilot/doctor/singer)



**J.  Who will help us for the following?**

baker    stationer    tailor    chemist    librarian

1.  To get clothes stitched  :  ___________________________

2. To buy medicines : ______________________

3. To buy bread : ______________________

4. To read books : ______________________

5. To buy pencils : ______________________

**K.  Match the community helpers with their places of work:**

farmer                              post office

policeman                           school

postman                             seashore

teacher                             fire station

fisherman                           police station

fireman                             field

**L.  Make a Doctor's Bag by following the below instructions:**

1.  Cut a chart paper into a rectangular shape

2.  Now, draw and colour a 'PLUS' sign on another paper

3.  Stick this paper on the rectangular chart paper

4.  Make a handle for the bag with a piece of chart paper

5.  Stick it on the top of the chart paper

6.  Now, write your name as Dr.____________________ on the bag

**M.  What does it mean to be honest? What would have happened if the woodcutter had not been honest? Discuss in class.**

# Teacher's Note
## UNIT 9

1. **Objectives:** Honesty, MCQs, Q&A, gap-fill, match people and places with work, conversation, word grid, words with the same meanings, odd word in group, Verbs+ing—how to use, making a doctor's bag.
2. **Listening and Speaking Skills:** Read aloud and focus on conversation between the characters. Ask students to read. Make this like a small skit in the class. Use the exercise on conversation to teach the students how to reply to the usual things that are asked of children. Pronunciation be corrected wherever required.
3. **Reading and Understanding:** Read the lesson aloud and explain it. Emphasise the honesty of the woodcutter. Do all the exercises orally first: the selection of the right word for the answer/gap-fill; and making suitable sentences in reply to the questions. Then get the students to write/ mark them in their books. Where sentences have to be written, put them on the blackboard, so they can transcribe them.
4. **Vocabulary:** Learn meanings and spellings of new words. Find words on the word-grid. Draw attention to words which mean the same or similar things, and find the odd word in each group. You can use other examples from real life. For example: 3 healthy foods, one junk food; 3 different types of seats [chair, sofa, bench], one fan, etc. What work is done by different people we observe in life. Correlate to the discussions you have had previously about the ambitions of the students.
5. **Grammar:** More about verbs and their form using Verb+ing. Make a classroom game of forming +ing verbs. Ask students to find words. Then, make them into small easy sentences.
6. **Writing Skills:** Continue to practise cursive writing. Also, make small sentences using the words we have learnt so far. Do this orally; write the sentences on the board and ask the students to transcribe them into their books.
7. **Activities:** Make a doctor's bag as suggested. Use an old shoe carton or any small cardboard container in which tea, etc. is bought. If students don't have any, then try some other craft using whatever material they may be able to get: a powder tin, a small cup or mug, or a thermocol tumbler.
8. **Values:** The value of honesty is very significant. This needs to be discussed with the students, because it is a core value that should last throughout life for them. Talk about honesty within the perspective of the students, without making it into a heavy lecture on morality.

# 10 The Summer Holidays

There are five main seasons in our country: Summer, Rainy season, Winter, Autumn and Spring.

Which is your favourite season? ________________________________

**There are some words and pictures given below. Encircle the ones that remind you of the summer season:**

shorts

snow

rain

ice cream

hot

sun

clouds

holidays

Six-year old Tim was very excited. It was the first day of the summer holidays. His cousins, Ben and Emily, were staying with him for the holidays.

Both Ben and Emily were eight years old. Tim wanted to play with them, but Ben said, "You are too young to play with us. Go and play with your own friends."

Tim was very upset and started crying. He wished that he was older so that Ben might play with him. Emily saw him crying and hugged him. She said, "Tim, don't feel so sad. I would love to play with you."

Tim felt much happier. He and Emily played hide and seek, tag and snakes and ladders all afternoon. They had so much fun.

In the evening, Ben returned home after playing with his friends. He was surprised to see Tim and Emily laughing and playing together. He went up to them and said, "Can I play with you, too?"

Emily replied, "We are in the middle of the game. Why don't you join us in the next game?"

So, Ben sat by the side. He felt upset that he had to wait, while they had so much fun. Slowly, he realised how Tim must have felt earlier. He was very sorry. Later that evening, he said 'sorry' to Tim and promised never to be rude and mean again.

The three cousins had a wonderful time that summer, playing and enjoying themselves together.

## A. Answer the following questions from the chapter:

1. How old was Ben?

   He was ________________________________.

2. What games did Tim and Emily play together?

   Tim and Emily played ________________________________.

3. Why did Ben not want to play with Tim?

   Ben said that Tim was too ________________________________.

4. Why did Emily not let Ben join the game?

   Emily did not let Ben join the game because

   ________________________________.

## B. Tick (✓) the correct answer:

1. Emily played with ____________ all day long.

   a. Ben ☐

   b. Tim ☐

2. Ben told Tim to play with ____________.

   a. his own friends ☐

   b. older children. ☐

3. Ben was upset in the evening because ____________.

   a. he had to wait while Ben and Emily were playing together. ☐

   b. he had hurt his knee. ☐

4. Ben and Emily visited Tim for the ____________.

   a. winter vacation. ☐

   b. summer holidays. ☐

**C.  Encircle the activities you enjoy during your summer holidays:**

playing cricket               swimming

going to school               reading stories

visiting relatives            wearing sweaters

studying                      drinking lemonade

playing in the park           ice skating

**D.  Unjumble the letters and name the following according to the clues:**

1.  A game we play indoors:

    D L U O          _____________________

2.  During vacation, we don't have to go here:

    S H O C O L      _____________________

3.  We should share our:

    Y T O S          _____________________

4.  Another word for vacation:

    H L O D I Y A    _____________________

5.  Before meals we should wash our:

    N D S H A        _____________________

## GRAMMAR

When we want to write about something that already happened, we add 'ed' to an action word. This is called the **simple past tense** because the action has already happened.

**For example :**

wash + ed = washed      climb + ed = climbed
start + ed = started      play  + ed = played

**E.   Use 'ed' form of the verbs to fill up the blanks:**

1.  Harry _______________ (call) his friend on the phone.

2.  Yesterday, I _______________ (wash) my hair.

3.  Tara _______________ (walk) home from school.

4.  Jake _______________ (brush) his teeth last night.

5.  Fran _______________ (help) her brother to finish his homework.

6.  Annie had _______________ (finish) her homework.

**F.   Change the 'today' sentences into 'yesterday' sentences. The first one has been done for you:**

1.  Hari pulls the curtains.
    <u>Hari pulled the curtains.</u>

2.  Sid packs his bag.

    _______________________________________________________.

3.  Dia enters the room.

    _______________________________________________________.

4.  I play with my friend.

   ___________________________________________________.

5.  The girl talks sweetly.

   ___________________________________________________.

6.  Heidi walks beautifully.

   ___________________________________________________.

**G.  Your teacher will speak out the following words from the story. Repeat the words after him/her:**

| | | |
|---|---|---|
| 1.  holiday | 2.  games | 3.  excited |
| 4.  promise | 5.  wonderful | 6.  rude |

**H.  Speaking politely:**

We should always talk politely to others.

If we want to ask for something, we should say, "Please".
If someone gives us something, we should say, "Thank you".
If we hurt someone or do something wrong, we should say, "Sorry".

Use these magic words to have a conversation with your partner. Use the hints given below.

a: "Could you pass me a pencil, please?"

b: "Yes, of course."

a: "Thank you very much."

b: "You are welcome."

You could use the following options to begin a conversation:

- Share a notebook
- Share lunch
- Share your toys
- Share your crayons

**I.** **Tick (✓) the correct option:**

1. We should share our toys and books with ________________________ .

   a. our friends

   b. no one

2. I feel happy when ________________________________ .

   a. I help my parents

   b. I lose my pencil box

3. We should ____________________ say 'thank you' and 'please'.

   a. never

   b. always

4. We should ________________________ before meals.

   a. wash our hands

   b. play outside

5. If it is raining outside, we should ____________________ .

   a. play indoor games, like ludo, snakes and ladders, etc.

   b. get angry

**J.** **Put a tick (✓) in front of good behaviour and a cross (✗) in front of bad behaviour:**

1. Cleaning your room ☐

2. Shouting at your friends ☐

3. Making your bed ☐

4. Snatching someone else's sweets ☐

5. Saying 'thank you' ☐

6. Wishing your teacher 'good morning' ☐

**K.** **Use the following words to make sentences:**

1. promise : _______________________________

2. wonderful : _______________________________

3. excited : _______________________________

4. holiday : _______________________________

**L.** **Rewrite the following sentences using the correct capital letters and full stops:**

1. raman is a good boy

   _______________________________________.

2. i have movie watched

   _______________________________________.

3. paul has a pet mouse

   _______________________________________.

4. mother has cooked lunch

   _______________________________________.

5. father is in mumbai today

   _______________________________________.

**M.** **Have you ever felt upset while playing with others? What made you feel upset? Share your story with the class.**

# Poem

## Hide and Seek

*Hide and seek around the park,*
*to find a special hiding place.*
*"1, 2, 3," behind a tree,*
*scampering here and there.*

*"4, 5, 6," too many sticks,*
*must seek another place to hide.*
*"7, 8, 9," next seeker's turn, not mine,*
*so I find a tree or bush to hide.*

*"10 !" the seeker calls out loud!*
*now begins the hunt, one by one.*
*Excitedly, quietly, waiting…*
*I'm found!*

*– Roger W. Hancock*

## A. Write 'True' or 'False':

1. We can play 'hide and seek' alone.  ____________

2. The seeker counts till ten before finding the others.  ____________

3. The game is played with sticks.  ____________

4. The game is over when everyone is found.  ____________

5. The person who hides is called the seeker.  ____________

## B. Solve the crossword using the clues given below:

| hockey | cricket | football |
| --- | --- | --- |
| hide and seek | racing | ludo |

**ACROSS**

2. A game where each person tries to run faster than the other
3. A game where we kick the ball
4. A popular board game
5. A game played with a bat and ball
6. India's national game

**DOWN**

1. A game where players hide, and the seeker has to find them

**'Has' and 'Have'**

'Have' is used with I, you and plural words. 'Has' is used with he, she and a singular word.

**For example:**    I have a pen.

She has a pencil.

We have to work hard.

## C. Fill up each blank with 'has' or 'have':

1. Anna and Sam ________________ many pens.

2. Tom ___________________ one brother.

3. Max ___________________ two books.

4. Harry and Peter ________________ bicycles.

**D.** **You have already learnt the different kinds of vowel sounds. Divide the words according to their sounds:**

| bun | sun | jug | tin | big | win | rag | hat | sat |
|-----|-----|-----|-----|-----|-----|-----|-----|-----|
| fog | fox | box | get | set | let | spoon | school | tool |

| 'a' sound | 'e' sound | 'i' sound | 'o' sound | 'oo' sound | 'u' sound |
|-----------|-----------|-----------|-----------|------------|-----------|
|  |  |  |  |  |  |
|  |  |  |  |  |  |
|  |  |  |  |  |  |

THINK AND TELL

**E.** **We all enjoy playing games. We play some games indoors, and some games outdoors. We can play some games by ourselves, while we need many players for other games. But no matter what the game is, we always have a great time playing:**

**Look at the games given here. Some games are played outdoors, while others can be played inside the house. Write 'I' for the Indoor games and 'O' for the Outdoor games:**

**F. Look at the pictures and name the games being played:**

(i)

(ii)

___________________________                    ___________________________

**G. Name three other games you enjoy playing:**

1. ___________________________

2. ___________________________

3. ___________________________

**H. What is your favourite game? Write a few sentences about it:**

___________________________________________________________

___________________________________________________________

___________________________________________________________

___________________________________________________________

___________________________________________________________

# Teacher's Note
## UNIT 10

1. **Objectives:** Listening, speaking, reading and writing. Q&A, gap-fill, making sentences, Using Capitals and punctuation. Unscramble words and do crosswords.Past Tense using +ed. Using has and have. Observe pictures and write sentences. Learning to separate vowel sounds. Spending time with family: Holidays. What are the seasons and seasonal things we see and use? Games we play. What is good and polite behaviour? Poem-Hide and Seek, T/F.

2. **Listening and Speaking Skills:** Learn all vowel sounds clearly and how to recognize them. Read aloud and ask the students to read words and sentences too. Correct the pronunciation where required. Converse using 'thank you', 'please', 'sorry', etc.

3. **Reading and Understanding:** Read aloud and explain the lesson and new words. Then do the gap-fill and questions and answers orally. Then, write the answers on the blackboard for students to transcribe. Reading, learning and reciting a poem. Answering questions on the poem.

4. **Vocabulary:** Words and their meanings. How they help with the crossword. Unscramble letters to make a word. This can be done with more examples from the class and home. Words with vowels: recognizing them and segregating them. Names of indoor and outdoor games. Seasons and the names of things we see or use in each season. Words used for polite behaviour.

5. **Grammar:** What are Capital letters used for? And basic punctuation—full stop, question mark. What happens when we talk about yesterday's actions? Verbs-past tense, Using +ed. Using has and have.

6. **Writing Skills:** Write sentences in answering questions, and make sentences with given words. Think and write about what you like to do as pastime. Continue to practise cursive writing.

7. **Activities:** Spending time with family. What do we do as pastime, apart from watching TV? What are indoor and outdoor games? Do we play any of them? What are the different holiday activities we can do with our families?

8. **Values:** We should spend some time every day with our family. There are chores to be done. Also, good behaviour begins at home. Why do we need to be well behaved? What constitutes good behavior—politeness, sharing, consideration for others? Need for playing and relaxing together. How to deal with 'feeling left out'. How to overcome that feeling by reaching out to help others and to share things with them. Try not to make others feel left out.

# **ASSESSMENT - 2**

## Read and Tell

A monkey climbed up a tree. He swung from one branch to another. He was very happy. He did not see the nest high up among the branches. A Myna bird was very frightened. Her little babies could not fly yet. She chirped loudly and so did her babies. The monkey stopped swinging and looked up. He saw the bird and the nest. He was a kind monkey. So, waving to the bird, he went off to another tree.

**A.  Answer these questions based on the above story:**

1.  Who was climbing up the tree?

    _______________________________________________________.

2.  What did the Myna bird do?

    _______________________________________________________.

3.  Where did the monkey go?

    _______________________________________________________.

4.  Where was the nest?

    _______________________________________________________.

**B.  Complete the action words by adding -ed:**

climb  _____________   frighten  _____________

chirp_____________   look  _____________

**C.  Look at the pictures and add the correct position words:**

1.  The puppy sat _____________________ the chair.

2.  The kitten climbed _________ the tree.

3. The clock is ___________ the wall.

4. The cheese is ________ the fridge.

5. The boy jumped ______________ the hurdle.

**D. Add the adjectives from the box to complete each sentence given below:**

> funny   kind   red   loud   big   fat

1. Sunita wore a __________________ dress.
2. The _______________ clown made everyone laugh.
3. The people were frightened of the ____________ elephant.
4. He told them to switch off the _____________ music.
5. It was a _______________ monkey.
6. Alex was a _______________ boy.

**E. Write the opposites of the following words:**

1. cruel        _______________________
2. sad          _______________________
3. low          _______________________
4. clean        _______________________
5. big          _______________________

6. hot             ______________________

7. short           ______________________

8. young           ______________________

9. foolish         ______________________

10. day            ______________________



**F.  Match the words of the two columns to make the compound words:**

| Column A | Column B | Compound Word |
|---|---|---|
| 1.  note | a.  box | ______________________ |
| 2.  paint | b.  cream | ______________________ |
| 3.  flower | c.  book | ______________________ |
| 4.  lamp | d.  pot | ______________________ |
| 5.  ice | e.  post | ______________________ |
| 6.  black | f.  board | ______________________ |
| 7.  air | g.  plane | ______________________ |
| 8.  birth | h.  day | ______________________ |
| 9.  class | i.  room | ______________________ |
| 10.  butter | j.  fly | ______________________ |

**G.  Answer these questions from the lessons you have read:**

1.  What did the foolish Raven lose?

______________________________________________________.

2.  Where did Tina and Fred throw the plates?

______________________________________________________.

3.  How did the monkey help the giraffe?

______________________________________________________.

4.  Why was the fairy happy with the woodcutter?

______________________________________________________.

| Lesson Theme | Reading | Think and Tell | Listening & Speaking | Writing | Vocabulary | Grammar | Activity / Life Skills |
|---|---|---|---|---|---|---|---|
| **Little Jimmy**<br>Friends, family and surroundings | Fill up the blanks, Tick the correct answers | Fill up the blanks | Difficult words from the lesson, 'a' words | Letters and vowels | Use given words to complete | Sentences | About Self |
| **The Old Woman Who Lived in a Shoe** | MCQs | Fill up the blanks | | Complete Sentences, True/False | | This/That, These/Those | Activity |
| **The Giraffe and the Monkey**<br>Helping one another | Fill up the blanks, True/False | Match animals to their homes | Difficult words from the lesson, 'e' words | Fill up the blanks | Fill up the blanks, Crossword | Nouns | Question to discuss in the Activity |
| **The Rainbow Story**<br>Colours | Complete sentences using hints | Fill up the blanks | Difficult words from the lesson, 'ch' words | Fill up the blanks | Match words to pictures | Articles, Use of a/an | Activity |
| **The Perfect House**<br>Jungle story | Write answers using given hints, Tick the correct answers | Match pictures to the words | Difficult words from the lesson, 'sh' words | Complete sentences, Number sentences to correct sequence picture-story | Crossword, Poem and MCQs | Naming words | Questions to discuss class |
| **The Mulberry Bush** | Complete sentences | Name activities in the picture | | | Crossword | One and many, Use of is/are | |
| **Heidi's Wonderful Day**<br>Exploring Nature | MCQs, Match names to the characters | Question to discuss in the class, Encircle the words | Difficult words from the lesson, 'oo' words | Make sentences with given words, Complete the poem write rhyming words | Make new words, Complete sentences after reading the poem | Action words | Questions to discuss in class |

# MODEL TEST PAPER ASSESSMENT-I

| Lesson Theme | Reading | Think and Tell | Listening & Speaking | Writing | Vocabulary | Grammar | Activity/ Life Skills |
|---|---|---|---|---|---|---|---|
| **The Raven and the Fox** — Classic Story | MCQs, True/False | Match the words to their meanings, Fill up the blanks with sounds | Difficult words from the lesson, 'ee' words | Complete the story with given hints | Match pictures to the words | Action words | Question to discuss in the class, Activity |
| **Everyone is Important** — Respect others | Complete Sentences, Write answers | Complete words, Match pictures to words | Difficult words from the lesson, Greetings | Make sentences using given hints | Fill up the blanks using opposites, Match the opposites | Prepositions | Activity |
| **Ice Cream Man** | Fill up the blanks, Rhyming words | Question to discuss in the class | | Compounds words | | | |
| **A Day in the Park** — Cleanliness | Fill up the blanks, Answer the questions | Fill up the blanks | Difficult words from the lesson | Complete Sentences | Crossword | Adjectives | Activity |
| **The Honest Woodcutter** — Honesty Pays | MCQ, Fill up the blanks, Answer the questions, | Match people to their professions, Name the professionals | Difficult words from the lesson, Conversation | | Encircle words with similar meanings | Use of 'ing' | Activity, Question to discuss in the class |
| **The Summer Holidays** | Complete the answers, MCQs | MCQs, Tick the correct answers | Difficult words from the lesson, Using Magic words | Make sentences with the given words, Punctuate and rewrite the words | Encircle names of activities, Unscramble | Past tense | Question to discuss in the class |
| **Hide and Seek** | True/False | Name the games, Mark the Indoor and Outdoor games | | | Crossword | Use of has/have | Segregate and write words with different vowel sounds |

**ASSESSMENT-II**

# Answers

## CHAPTER 1
### COME ALONG

1. Puppy    2. Four    3. Blue

**A.** 1. first    2. puppy    3. ball
4. park    5. bag    6. Benny

**B.** 1. ✗   2. ✔   3. ✗   4. ✔   5. ✗

**C.** 1. pencil   2. red   3. bicycle   4. love

**D.** 1. WATER   2. SUN   3. BOOTS
4. CLOUD   5. PENCIL

**E.** 1. ✗   2. ✔   3. ✔   4. ✗   5. ✔   6. ✗

**H.** 1. park   2. hospital   3. school   4. learn

**I.** • B   F   I   M   O   T   Y
  • A B C D E F G H I J K L M N O P Q R S T U V W X Y Z
  • e   f   k   l   p   q   v   x   z
  • a b c d e f g h i j k l m n o p q r s t u v w x y z

**J.** fox     raven     cow
    elephant     tiger     butterfly

### POEM

**A.** 1. shoe    2. her children    3. bread

**B.** 1. This, That    2. This, That    3. This, That

**C.** 1. That    2. This    3. Those
4. These    5. That    6. This

**D.** 1. ✔   2. ✗   3. ✔   4. ✗   5. ✔   6. ✗   7. ✔

**F.** False    True    True    False    True

**G.** Igloo    Hut    Bungalow

## CHAPTER 2
### COME ALONG

Monkey- 2     Rabbit- 1     Fox- 3
Tiger- 4     Elephant- 5

**A.** 1. giraffe    2. top    3. alone    4. help

**B.** 1. False    2. True    3. True
4. True    5. False

**C.**

| M | O | E | G | M | J | B | I |
|---|---|---|---|---|---|---|---|
| A | P | P | L | E | G | A | U |
| N | W | X | E | L | H | N | B |
| G | R | A | P | E | S | A | X |
| O | F | N | A | C | A | N | Q |
| R | W | P | P | T | B | A | E |
| T | Q | V | U | Y | O | H | Y |
| P | A | P | A | Y | A | N | L |

**D.** 1. trees   2. monkey   3. two   4. birds   5. tall

**E.** b - bear, ball    c - cat, cap    s - ship, shoe
t - tiger, truck    r - rabbit, rat

**F.**

| Person | Place | Animal | Thing |
|---|---|---|---|
| Mary | France | bear | book |
| Reena | Delhi | horse | grapes |
| Matthew | London | camel | bag |
| Rohan | Mumbai | tiger | shirt |

**I.** dog -     cat -     sheep - 
horse -    duck - 

**J.** 2. Jenny is darker than Sam.
    Sam is fairer than Jenny.
3. Uncle Ben is older than Milly.
    Milly is younger than Uncle Ben.

**K.** books - ✔   shoes- ✔   clothes- ✔   bag - ✔   comb - ✔

## CHAPTER 3
### COME ALONG

1. Rain    2. Umbrella    3. Boy    4. Clouds

**A.** 1. useful    2. Green    3. water    4. Red
5. power    6. sun    7. seven    8. rain
9. Pink    10. Orange

**B.** 1. Rain
2. VIOLET    YELLOW    INDIGO    ORANGE
    BLUE    RED    GREEN

**C.** - duckling    - roses
    - kangaroo    - carrots

**D.** 2. An    3. an    4. a    5. an

**E.** 2. a book    3. an ice-cream    4. a dog

**H.** 2. toothbrush   3. pencil   4. notebook   5. shoes

**I.** 1. eat pizza    2. the park
3. is beautiful    4. is sleeping

## CHAPTER 4
### COME ALONG

1. Study Room    2. Bedroom
3. Living Room    4. Bathroom

**A.** 1. stag and tiger    2. tiger    3. stag
4. tiger    5. dry grass
6. they got shocked

**B.** 1. ✘  2. ✔  3. ✘  4. ✔  5. ✘

**C.**

**ACROSS**

3. clean    4. kitchen    5. dog    6. bed

**DOWN**

1. shelter    2. dining

**D.** 1. b    2. c    3. a    4. b

**E.** football, Shyam, Anita, sandwiches, lunch, park, pond, fish, bread, fish, pond, fish, edge, bread

**H.**

 - hut     - spider's web

 - nest     - kennel

**J.** 1. big    2. hole in the wall    3. the hole
4. scared    5. hole

**K.**

## POEM

**A.** 1. early    2. wash, comb    3. brush    4. clothes

**B.**

| m | o | r | n | i | n | g | f |
|---|---|---|---|---|---|---|---|
| i | z | a | s | r | e | r | h |
| b | a | t | h | y | a | e | e |
| r | b | i | l | e | t | s | a |
| u | w | q | r | g | b | c | l |
| s | l | e | e | p | k | v | t |
| h | m | b | d | e | s | e | h |
| r | c | l | e | a | n | w | y |



**C.** **Singular** - chair, goat, mat, pen
**Plural** - ants, hens, songs, apples

**D.** 1. are    2. is    3. are    4. is
5. are    6. is    7. are    8. is, is

**E.** waking up    taking a bath    brushing teeth
combing hair    wearing clothes

## CHAPTER 5

**A.** 1. b    2. a    3. b    4. a

**B.**

 - Heidi     - grandfather

 - goat     - Peter

**C.** 1. colourful    2. fly    3. caterpillars
4. high    5. summer

**D.** 2. C, D    3. B, D    4. L, B    5. H, T

**E.** 2. colours    3. fly    4. sings    5. listens

**F.** 1. combs    2. reads    3. eats
4. washes    5. barks

**J.** tree, sandwiches, birds, ball, games, frisbee, friends

**K.** 1. That mountain looks very beautiful.
2. I am feeling hungry.
3. I saw a bad dream last night.
4. There is plenty of food in the fridge.

**L.** sky, me, sight

**M.** 1. ring, wing    2. plate, gate    3. noon, boon

## ASSESSMENT - 1

**A.** 1. birdhouse    2. Mohit's Dad    3. tree

**B.** 1. blue    2. brown    3. yellow    4. green
5. blue    6. red

**C.** 1. an    2. An    3. a    4. an    5. a    6. an

**D.** 1. Things    2. Animals    3. Places    4. Persons

| Person | Place | Animal | Thing |
|---|---|---|---|
| Mohit | Temple | Dog | Chair |
| Heidi | City | Cat | Table |
| Mona | Post Office | Sparrow | Pencil |
| Raman | Village | Lion | Notebook |

**E.** 1. sparrow    2. tree    3. chocolate

**F.** 1. t t    2. e e    3. e e    4. l l    5. t t

**G.** 1. eat    2. writes    3. walk

**H.** 1. is    2. are    3. are    4. is

**I.** 1. The old woman lived in the shoe.
2. Peter was Heidi's friend.

# CHAPTER 6

**A.** 1. a 2. b 3. a 4. b 5. b

**B.** 1. True 2. False 3. True
4. False 5. True

**C.**

| foal | calf | puppy | joey | kitten |
| --- | --- | --- | --- | --- |
| ↓ | ↓ | ↓ | ↓ | ↓ |
| horse | cow | dog | kangaroo | cat |

2. kitten 3. joey 4. foal 5. calf

**D.** 1. Rohit is sleeping. 2. Bina is eating.
3. Veena is playing. 4. Shiv is jumping.

**G.** 1. pitter-patter 2. splash
3. croak 4. clip-clop

**H.** vain=proud    above=over    lovely=nice
sad=upset    below=under

**I.** 2. drink water from the pot.    3. into the pot.
4. drinking the water.

# CHAPTER 7
## COME ALONG

Desert    Forest    Hills    Ocean

**A.** 1. desert 2. sand 3. hawk 4. no one

**B.** 1. desert 2. no other tree was there in the forest.
3. The hawk came to sit
4. him shade from the hot sun.

**C.** rich=poor    sad=happy    weak=strong
tight=loose    bright=dark

**D.** 1. hot, cold 2. tall, short 3. old, young
4. early, late 5. wise, foolish

**E.** 1. in 2. on 3. under 4. under 5. in

**F.** 1. in 2. on 3. in 4. on 5. in

**I.** 1. banyan 2. oak 3. pine
4. bamboo 5. palm 6. neem

**J.**

- leaf
- roots
- branches
- trunk

**K.** 1. The bird sits on the tree.
2. The tree grows in the park.
3. The dog barks loudly.
4. The cat sleeps on the sidewalk.
5. The children play in the park.

**L.**

## POEM

**A.** 1. summer 2. little cart
3. cone with mound 4. honeybees

**B.** 2. might : sight 3. drink : pink
4. peas : bees 5. hounds : mounds

**D.**

| Column A | Column B | Compound Word |
| --- | --- | --- |
| news | paper | newspaper |
| down | stairs | downstairs |
| arm | chair | armchair |
| earth | quake | earthquake |
| air | port | airport |
| rain | coat | raincoat |
| note | book | notebook |
| black | board | blackboard |
| police | man | policeman |

**E.**

| airport | bag | table | daytime | mail | time |
| --- | --- | --- | --- | --- | --- |
| hand | bookcase | call | haircut | earthquake | man |
| wheelchair | earphone | handbag | band | fish | fireplace |
| ice | hand | key | houseboat | house | lady |
| gateway | shelf | land | fire | notebook | cat |

# CHAPTER 8
## COME ALONG

1. play ludo 2. play football
3. watch television 4. solve puzzles

**A.** 1. car 2. paper 3. apples 4. ran
5. stories 6. stars 7. doll

**B.** 1. Tina and her family went for a picnic at the park.
2. They ate sandwiches and salad.
3. The stars began to come out when it was dark.
4. They threw the paper plates into the dustbin.
5. They played 'tag'.

**C.**

| f | o | o | d | d | t | e |
| --- | --- | --- | --- | --- | --- | --- |
| r | t | p | a | p | e | r |
| u | v | n | b | c | w | g |
| i | r | u | u | j | o | s |
| t | a | t | p | l | o | w |
| e | i | s | h | a | d | e |
| a | r | t | i | j | h | d |

**D.** 1. tall  2. pretty  3. short  4. clean  5. brown

**E.** 1. long, short, curly    2. big, small, old, clean
3. sad, happy, pretty, hungry  4. tall, leafy
5. hot, tasty

**G.** 1. Sunday  2. seven  3. Thursday
4. Tuesday  5. Monday

**H.** zoo    elephant    neck    leaves
birds    sandwiches    evening    best

# CHAPTER 9

## COME ALONG

A woodcutter cuts wood
1. Pencil    2. Table    3. Door

**A.** 1. b    2. a    3. b

**B.** 1. axe    2. gold    3. happy    4. honest

**C.** 1. The woodcutter lived in a village near the forest.
2. A fairy from the river appeared in front of the woodcutter.
3. The fairy gave all three axes—gold, silver & iron—to the woodcutter.

**D.** 1. labour  2. correct  3. speak  4. jungle

**E.** 1. CARPENTER    2. JOKER    3. PLUMBER

**F.** 1. singing  2. calling  3. sleeping  4. cooking
5. talking  6. playing  7. eating

**G.** 1. sleeping  2. crying  3. trying  4. falling
5. licking  6. wearing

**J.** farmer  → field        policeman → police station
postman  → post office    teacher  → school
fisherman → boat          fireman  → fire station

**K.** 1. tailor  2. chemist  3. baker
4. librarian  5. stationer

# CHAPTER 10

## COME ALONG

shorts    ice cream    sun    holidays

**A.** 1. eight years old.
2. hide and seek, tag, snakes and ladders.
3. young to play with him.
4. She and Tim were in the middle of a game.

**B.** 1. b  2. a  3. a  4. b

**C.** playing cricket    swimming    reading stories
drinking lemonade    playing in the park    ice skating

**D.** 1. LUDO  2. SCHOOL  3. TOYS
4. HOLIDAY  5. HANDS

**E.** 1. called  2. washed  3. walked  4. brushed
5. helped  6. finished

**F.** 2. Sid packed his bag.  3. Dia entered the room.
4. I played with my friend.  5. The girl talked sweetly.
6. Heidi walked beautifully.

**I.** 1. a  2. a  3. b  4. a  5. a

**J.** 1. ✔  2. ✘  3. ✔  4. ✘  5. ✔  6. ✔

**K.** 1. I promise to help you learn English.
2. This was a wonderful trip.
3. I am excited for my holidays.
4. I need a holiday.

**L.** 1. Raman is a good boy.  2. Have you seen Shiela?
3. Paul has a pet mouse.  4. Mother has cooked lunch.
5. Father is in Mumbai today.

## POEM

**A.** 1. False  2. True  3. False  4. True  5. False

**B.**
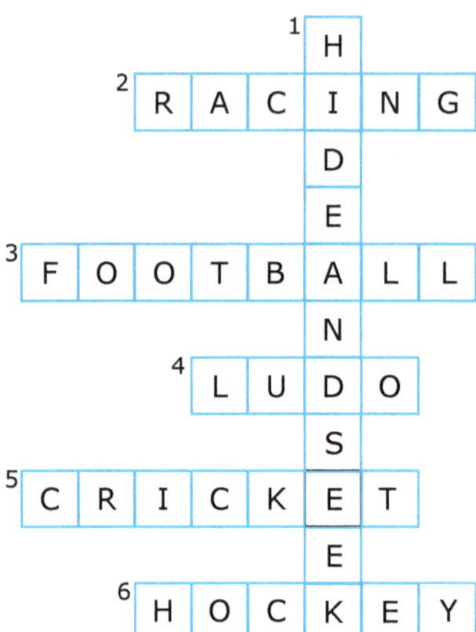


**C.** 1. have    2. has    3. has    4. have

**D.**

| 'a' sound | 'e' sound | 'i' sound | 'o' sound | 'oo' sound | 'u' sound |
| --- | --- | --- | --- | --- | --- |
| hat | get | tin | fog | spoon | bun |
| rag | set | big | fox | school | sun |
| sat | let | win | box | tool | jug |

**F.** 1. Football  2. Video Games

## ASSESSMENT - 2

**A.** 1. A monkey was climbing up the tree.
2. The Myna bird was frightened, so she chirped loudly.
3. The monkey went off to another tree.
4. The nest was high up among the branches of the tree.

**B.** 1. climbed  2. frightened  3. chirped  4. looked

**C.** 1. under  2. on  3. on  4. in  5. over

**D.** 1. red  2. funny  3. large  4. loud
5. kind  6. fat

**E.** 1. kind  2. happy  3. high  4. dirty  5. small
6. cold  7. long  8. old  9. smart  10. night

**F.** Compound words
1. notebook    2. paintbox    3. flowerpot
4. lamppost    5. icecream    6. blackboard
7. airplane    8. birthday    9. classroom
10. butterfly

**G.** 1. The foolish Raven lost his slice of bread.
2. Tina and Fred threw the plates into the dustbin.
3. The monkey climbed on the back of the giraffe and plucked the fruit.
4. The fairy was happy with the woodcutter because he was honest.